Michael Phelps

Other books in the People in the News series:

Maya Angelou
Jennifer Aniston
Tyra Banks
David Beckham
Beyoncé
Fidel Castro
Kelly Clarkson
Hillary Clinton
Miley Cyrus
Hilary Duff
Zac Efron
Brett Favre
50 Cent
Al Gore
Tony Hawk
Salma Hayek
LeBron James
Jay-Z
Derek Jeter
Steve Jobs
Dwayne Johnson
Angelina Jolie
Jonas Brothers
Kim Jong Il

Coretta Scott King
Ashton Kutcher
Tobey Maguire
John McCain
Barack Obama
Danica Patrick
Nancy Pelosi
Queen Latifah
Daniel Radcliffe
Condoleezza Rice
Rihanna
J.K. Rowling
Shakira
Tupac Shakur
Will Smith
Gwen Stefani
Ben Stiller
Hilary Swank
Justin Timberlake
Usher
Kanye West
Oprah Winfrey

Michael Phelps

by Barbara Sheen

LUCENT BOOKS
A part of Gale, Cengage Learning

GALE
CENGAGE Learning™

Detroit • New York • San Francisco • New Haven, Conn • Waterville, Maine • London

GALE
CENGAGE Learning

LIBRARY OF CONGRESS CATALOGING-IN-PUBLICATION DATA

Sheen, Barbara.
  Michael Phelps / by Barbara Sheen.
    p. cm. -- (People in the news)
  Includes bibliographical references and index.
  ISBN 978-1-4205-0282-4 (hardcover)
  1. Phelps, Michael, 1985--Juvenile literature. 2. Swimmers--United States--Biography--Juvenile literature. I. Title.
  GV838.P54S54 2010
  797.2'1092--dc22
  [B]
                                                                    2009053265

Lucent Books
27500 Drake Rd.
Farmington Hills, MI 48331

ISBN-13: 978-1-4205-0282-4
ISBN-10: 1-4205-0282-4

Printed in the United States of America
1 2 3 4 5 6 7 14 13 12 11 10

Printed by Bang Printing, Brainerd, MN, 1st Ptg., 07/2010

Contents

ame and celebrity are alluring. People are drawn to those who walk in fame's spotlight, whether they are known for great accomplishments or for notorious deeds. The lives of the famous pique public interest and attract attention, perhaps because their experiences seem in some ways so different from, yet in other ways so similar to, our own.

Newspapers, magazines, and television regularly capitalize on this fascination with celebrity by running profiles of famous people. For example, television programs such as *Entertainment Tonight* devote all of their programming to stories about entertainment and entertainers. Magazines such as *People* fill their pages with stories of the private lives of famous people. Even newspapers, newsmagazines, and television news frequently delve into the lives of well-known personalities. Despite the number of articles and programs, few provide more than a superficial glimpse at their subjects.

Lucent's People in the News series offers young readers a deeper look into the lives of today's newsmakers, the influences that have shaped them, and the impact they have had in their fields of endeavor and on other people's lives. The subjects of the series hail from many disciplines and walks of life. They include authors, musicians, athletes, political leaders, entertainers, entrepreneurs, and others who have made a mark on modern life and who, in many cases, will continue to do so for years to come.

These biographies are more than factual chronicles. Each book emphasizes the contributions, accomplishments, or deeds that have brought fame or notoriety to the individual and shows how that person has influenced modern life. Authors portray their subjects in a realistic, unsentimental light. For example, Bill Gates—the cofounder and chief executive officer of the software giant Microsoft—has been instrumental in making personal computers the most vital tool of the modern age. Few dispute his business savvy, his perseverance, or his technical expertise, yet critics say he is ruthless in his dealings with competitors and driven more by his desire to maintain Microsoft's dominance in the computer industry than by an interest in furthering technology.

In these books, young readers will encounter inspiring stories about real people who achieved success despite enormous obstacles. Oprah Winfrey—the most powerful, most watched, and wealthiest woman on television today—spent the first six years of her life in the care of her grandparents while her unwed mother sought work and a better life elsewhere. Her adolescence was colored by promiscuity, pregnancy at age fourteen, rape, and sexual abuse.

Each author documents and supports his or her work with an array of primary and secondary source quotations taken from diaries, letters, speeches, and interviews. All quotes are footnoted to show readers exactly how and where biographers derive their information and provide guidance for further research. The quotations enliven the text by giving readers eyewitness views of the life and accomplishments of each person covered in the People in the News series.

In addition, each book in the series includes photographs, annotated bibliographies, timelines, and comprehensive indexes. For both the casual reader and the student researcher, the People in the News series offers insight into the lives of today's newsmakers—people who shape the way we live, work, and play in the modern age.

"Dream It, Believe It, Work at It, Go for It"

On August 17, 2008, Michael Phelps stood on the Olympic podium in Beijing, China, for the final time during the 2008 Olympics. He was about to receive his eighth gold medal of the games. Never before had an athlete won as many gold medals in a single Olympics.

Before the games began many people said such a feat was impossible. Phelps was determined to prove them wrong. From an early age, he had dreamed of doing something no one else had ever done. Now he had. "If you put a limit on anything, you put a limit on how far you can go. . . . If you think about doing the unthinkable, you can," he insists. "Anything is possible."[1]

But Phelps did more than dream. He planned, he worked, and he persevered. It took a combination of many different elements for him to succeed.

Natural Ability and Physical Advantages

Natural talent was one of these elements. Athleticism runs in Phelps's family. His mother was a high school cheerleader. His father was a college football star and later went on to try out for the Washington Redskins. Phelps's sisters, Hillary and Whitney, were outstanding swimmers. Whitney swam in the World Championships in 1994. If injuries had not sidetracked her, she probably would have made it to the Olympics. Phelps was fortunate to inherit athletic talent. Without it, he could not have reached the point where he is today.

Phelps's body shape also helped him. He is 6 feet 4 inches (1.93m) tall with a wingspan of 6 feet 7 inches (1.97m), which allows him to take fewer and longer strokes than most other swimmers. He has a long torso in relation to his legs. This makes him more aerodynamic than someone with a short torso and long legs. And, he has large hands and feet, which act like paddles. He is also extremely flexible, which helps him to move fluidly through the water.

This combination of physical traits is ideal for a swimmer. According to journalist Vicki Michaelis, "In the water his short legs, with his double-jointed knees and pliable ankles attached to size 14 feet, help him undulate [roll] like a dolphin. His long arms,

U.S. swimmer Michael Phelps made history for winning the most gold medals in a single Olympics when he took eight at the 2008 Summer Olympics in Beijing.

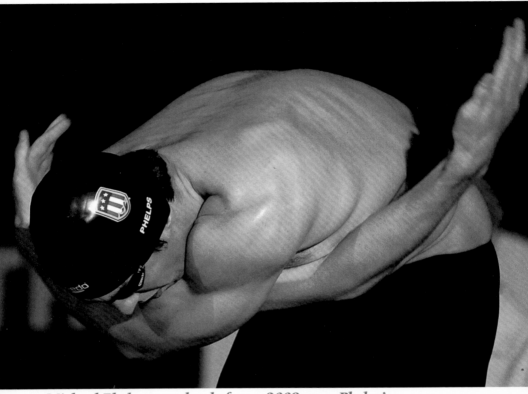

Michael Phelps stretches before a 2009 race. Phelps's flexibility assists him in moving fluidly through the water.

combined with the flexibility of his shoulders and elbows, extend the reach of his strokes, which are powerful and rhythmic."[2]

The Will to Win

Phelps's competitive nature also played a key role in his achievement. He has always hated to lose. Both his maternal grandmother and his father encouraged him to be competitive. He recalls: "If I was playing sports, no matter what it was, my father's direction was simple: 'Go hard and remember, good guys finish second.' That didn't mean that you were supposed to be a jerk, but it did mean that you were there to compete as hard as you could."[3]

Not only does Phelps compete against other swimmers, he competes against himself. Each time he races, he wants to better his own time. Even when he wins a race, if he does not beat his personal best time he is unsatisfied. Michael, according to his mother, "likes to raise the bar for himself and he is never one to be satisfied with having climbed a mountain or two; he needs an entire mountain range to conquer."[4] And, when others say he can't do something, it increases his determination to prove them wrong.

Hard Work

Even with his talent, physical advantages, and determination to win, Phelps had to work extremely hard to make his dreams come true. "Nothing in life is easy," he says. "You can't wake up one day, announce you're going to do something and expect to be a success. . . . You have to put time and energy and whatever you've got into it."[5]

In the six years before the 2008 Olympics, Phelps swam a total of 12,480 miles (20,084km), which is about the distance from the North Pole to the South Pole. Since then, he swims between four to six hours a day, racking up 30 to 50 miles (48 to 80km) per week. Plus, he cross-trains by riding a stationary bike, practicing yoga, lifting weights, and doing push-ups, sit-ups, and pull-ups. "I do about four or five varieties of pushups, 50 to 100 at a time, several types of sit-ups and crunches, usually around 500 or more each day; and I do up to five sets of eight pull-ups increasing the weight during each set,"[6] he explains.

Nor, does he take time off. There are no holidays on his calendar. Between 1998 and 2003, he missed only one day of training—the day his wisdom teeth were removed. In the year before the 2008 Olympics, he did not miss a single day. According to journalist Mike Celizic, "Very few of us can conceive of the level of work and dedication he put into winning those 8 gold medals."[7]

Strong Support

The support of his family and coach were also instrumental in Phelps's achieving his dreams. His mother drove him to and from practice twice a day for years. As a single parent, she often held down two jobs to help pay for membership at the North Baltimore Aquatic Club (NBAC) where Phelps trained. And, she never missed a swim meet. He always knew she was in the stands supporting him. She also supported him when he had problems in school, working with him to meet the challenges his learning differences posed. "For everything she's done for me growing up . . . I owe her the world,"[8] Phelps says.

Debbie Phelps congratulates her son Michael at the 2008 Summer Olympics in Beijing. Debbie Phelps has always been a strong support system for her son.

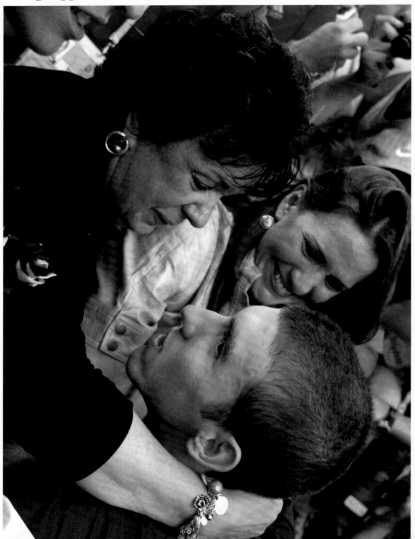

His sisters helped him too. They went to his swim meets and looked after him at home while his mother was working. They inspired him with their own swimming careers. Indeed, the family likes to call themselves "Team Phelps."

Phelps's coach, Bob Bowman, was also instrumental in Phelps's success. Early on, he recognized Phelps's potential. Despite the fact that Phelps was often difficult to coach, Bowman never gave up on him. Nor did he ever tell Phelps that his dreams were impossible.

Phelps is the first to admit that his dreams would not have come true without the many people that helped him. But even with his eight gold medals, he has not stopped dreaming. He never will. "You can do anything you want," he maintains. "You just have to dream it, believe it, work at it, go for it."[9] That is exactly what he has done, and what he is still doing.

Chapter 1

A Safe Haven

Michael Fred Phelps was born on June 30, 1985, in Towson, Maryland, to Debbie and Fred Phelps. Debbie was a teacher and Fred was a state trooper. Michael had two sisters, seven-year-old Hilary and five-year-old Whitney.

Michael's childhood was not easy. His parents divorced when he was young; he was frequently teased and bullied, and he struggled with attention deficit hyperactivity disorder (ADHD). Its symptoms—restlessness, impulsiveness, and inattentiveness—negatively impacted his behavior, his schoolwork, and his social life. The swimming pool provided him with a safe haven. In the water he forgot his problems.

Always Active

Even before he was born, Michael was active. According to his mother, in the last month of her pregnancy, he was always kicking the side of her stomach. His need to be moving became even more apparent as he grew. "He was a bundle of energy from the moment I first held him in my arms," Debbie Phelps recalls. "Besides being so loving, sweet, funny, and happy, he also had a natural ability to put himself in the middle of the action, no matter what it was—a trait that I suppose hasn't changed much since then."[10]

His high energy level often caused problems. His behavior during meal times is an example. When he was not occupied with eating, he played with the utensils and the food. "I was a handful at the dinner table, because I always had to do something with my hands. In my middle fingers I liked to twirl pens and pencils, but if they weren't available at dinner, I might try to substitute a saltshaker or a steak knife. I should have known I couldn't twirl a glass of milk." According to Phelps, "Until food arrived, it was up to my mom to keep me away from anything that could break, spill, cause bodily harm. . . . Once I was finished eating my food, I used to play with it. . . . I simply never could sit still. I made faces at cameras, answered questions with questions, climbed on things that weren't meant for climbing."[11]

Reckless Behavior

Added to this, he often acted recklessly. For instance, on one occasion the family was eating at a Mexican restaurant. Michael's parents warned him to be careful with the hot sauce. Ignoring their warning, Michael drowned his food in the sauce, then felt as if his mouth were on fire. He screamed for water, and then

Michael Phelps was born in Towson, Maryland, near Baltimore. The town named a street after him to celebrate his Olympic achievements.

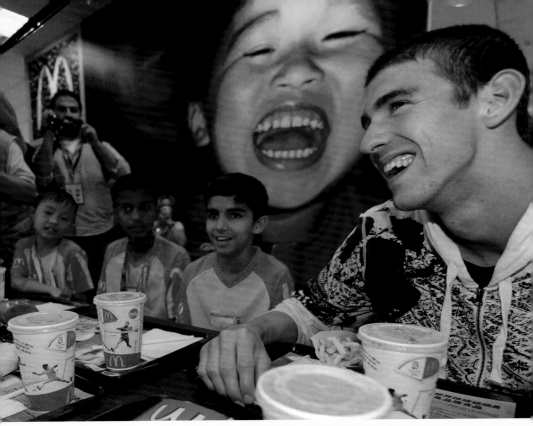

Michael Phelps eats lunch with children in Beijing during the 2008 Summer Olympics. Phelps was known for his mischievous antics at the supper table as a child.

drank so much, so fast, that it spurted out of his nose and mouth and spilled all over his body.

On another occasion his recklessness put him in danger. When he was two years old, his parents warned him to stay away from Thadeus, a large dog the family had rescued. The dog was neither used to toddlers nor was it trained yet. Despite his parents' warnings, Michael went into the dog's pen. Thadeus picked Michael up, dragged him through the dirt, and tossed him in the air like a rubber toy. Although Michael was not badly hurt, he had to get a series of painful rabies shots afterward. "Of course my parents warned me to be careful of Thadeus," Phelps recalls, "but parental warnings didn't usually stop me from experimenting with danger or discomfort."[12]

Trouble in School

Michael's recklessness and inability to sit still caused problems for him at school as well. To make matters worse, he had trouble focusing his attention. His thoughts jumped from one thing to another, and he was easily distracted. Plus, he lacked self-control. He blurted out answers, annoyed the other children, and asked countless questions. When things did not go his way, he became easily agitated, which caused him to cry, lose his temper, or have tantrums. His behavior distracted the other students and made it difficult for his teachers to do their job.

Michael's behavior was characteristic of a child with ADHD. Behavior modification therapy and/or medication help to control the disorder. But Michael's condition was not diagnosed until he was nine years old. Before then, he was frequently reprimanded for behavior that he was unable to manage, which frustrated him and lowered his self-esteem. Even after he gained more control over the condition, he struggled academically. Debbie Phelps recalls: "I heard

Michael Phelps was diagnosed with attention deficit hyperactivity disorder (ADHD) when he was nine. Children with this disorder find it difficult to focus on school work.

ADHD

ADHD is a medical condition characterized by distractibility, inattentiveness, restlessness, and impulsivity. The exact cause of ADHD is unknown. Scientists think that the brains of individuals with ADHD have chemical, structural, and/or functional differences from those of other people. The cause of these differences has not been established.

Many people with ADHD have the ability to hyperfocus. When individuals hyperfocus, they enter a state of extreme concentration in which they become so thoroughly engrossed in an activity that they completely block out all other thoughts and distractions. Hyperfocus usually occurs when individuals are performing an enjoyable activity. It is possible that Michael Phelps goes into a state of hyperfocus while he is swimming.

a range of comments from Michael's teachers about issues that later led to a diagnosis of ADHD. The comments were as mild as Michael has a hard time sitting still, to . . . his inability to focus and maintain attention is disruptive to the classroom and there is a possibility that difficulties will lie ahead of you."[13] One teacher predicted that Michael would never be able to focus on anything, while another insisted that he would never be a success.

Picked On

Michael's troubles did not end in the classroom. Because of his ADHD, he had trouble making eye contact and focusing on conversations. He often had to ask people to repeat themselves, which other children found peculiar. Although he wanted to fit in, other students thought he was odd. Socially, he was frequently teased and bullied.

His classmates knew just what to tease him about that would hurt him the most. He had big ears, which made him extremely self-conscious. He tried to hide them with a baseball cap, but the cap only made his ears more obvious. In addition, he had huge hands and feet, and a tall gangly body. Even though he was an excellent athlete, because of his long arms and short legs, he appeared very awkward. And he spoke with a lisp, which got worse when he was upset. The other children pulled and flicked his ears, tossed his cap around like a rubber ball, made fun of his long arms, and laughed at his lisp. When he reacted to their teasing by losing his temper, he often got in trouble. He was suspended from the school bus more than once for punching his tormentors. He recalls: "I just remember in middle school . . . kids flicking my ears. I remember in elementary school I'd have my hat thrown off the bus or I'd get made fun of. . . . The cool kids would always try to sit in the back, so I used to always try to sit in the back of the bus and could never do that, and if I tried to, that's when my hat would get thrown out the window. I remember yeah, it wasn't fun at the time."[14]

Divorce

Things at home were not going well either. Fred and Debbie Phelps did not have a happy marriage. When Michael was seven years old, his parents separated. They divorced shortly thereafter. Michael had been close to his father. The two shared a passion for sports, video games, and fishing. At first Michael could not accept that his father had moved out. Despite what his mother said, he waited for his father to come home. "I don't know if I had ever heard the words 'separation' or 'divorce' before," he explains. "Parents are always together. There is a mom and there is a dad and they will always be there to look after kids like me, to teach us, guide us, pat us on the back, have all the answers because parents just know these things, and they basically tell us what's what. I heard my mom explain to me that my dad really wasn't going to live with us anymore, but it didn't make sense. Dad must have gone out to get something."[15]

Michael soon realized that his father was really gone. What made things worse was that after the divorce Fred had little contact with his children. He rarely called, visited, or attended their

After his parents' divorce, young Michael no longer had the close bond with his father like this son and father have.

swim meets. In fact, when Phelps broke his first world record in 2001, his father did not call to congratulate him. To this day, Michael does not like to talk about his father or their relationship.

Whitney helped fill the void Fred left by being Michael's pal. "Michael and I spent a lot of time together," she explains.

> In our younger years, I remember going rollerblading and playing hoops with him and teaching him how to mow the grass. I took him under my wing, because my mom being a single parent took a lot. She was a teacher, so in the summers she took summer jobs to make ends meet. A lot of times, Michael and I would bum around together, going to the pool or hanging around the house. He would often go off and play with friends, or play video games. During those times and for school I'd make him breakfast, get him on the bus—just caring for him.[16]

Adding Structure

Debbie Phelps, too, did all that she could to help Michael cope with his problems. When he was nine years old, she had him tested for ADHD. Once he was diagnosed, Michael took medication on school days. The medication helped him to sit still and concentrate in class more easily.

Debbie took other steps to modify Michael's behavior and help him cope. She helped him with his homework and worked with him to develop methods to focus his attention and manage his time. For example, she kept a task list posted on the refrigerator for Michael. He had to do a list of chores in an allotted period of time before he could go to swim practice or play outside with his friends. When he completed a task, his mother gave him a sticker. This added structure to his life. And it helped him to focus on one activity at a time, which is often difficult for people with ADHD, who tend to move from one project to the next without finishing what they start. It also helped him learn how to manage his time, which is another problem for people with ADHD. With the help of Michael's sisters, Debbie also watched what he ate. She felt that too much junk food made him more hyperactive. "Kids need structure. Kids need consistency," Debbie Phelps explains. "I don't care if they have ADHD or not, they have to have those parameters [boundaries] in order to be successful. . . . Our family became a team, and the girls paid attention to Michael's eating habits. We also observed time restrictions on some activities to teach him time management, and he began making choices so that he could use his time more wisely, just as he would at the pool. Michael has mental toughness, but he never used to be able to focus."[17]

Debbie also tried to help him set goals and make positive choices. She taught him that, if he wanted something, he had to focus on it and work hard to get it. He could not let his emotions or his temper get in the way. The two did visualization exercises in which Michael envisioned a tense situation and how he could best handle it.

By forming the letter "C" with her fingers, she developed a symbol to help him manage his emotions in public places. The "C" stood for composure. Debbie often flashed him the signal from the stands at swimming meets to remind him to be a good sport. When he was young, if he lost a race, he often tore off his goggles and threw them across the pool deck in anger. Seeing his mom making a "C" helped him to control himself.

Into the Pool

Debbie also enrolled Michael in sports activities such as lacrosse, baseball, basketball, and soccer, which provided him with an outlet for his high energy and a chance to be successful. According to Hilary Phelps, "Michael was awesome at playing all sports. He was fast on his feet and had a lot of energy, so he could cover that lacrosse field like no other. Michael liked to win, so he always gave it his best."[18]

When Michael was seven years old, Debbie enrolled him in swimming lessons. His sisters were already swimming competitively. Although he did not know how to swim, Michael had spent a lot of time around swimming pools. From the time he was a toddler, his mother had taken him to his sisters' swim practices and meets. He spent many hours playing in the stands and watching his sisters swim. Debbie had no thought of Michael swimming competitively. She wanted him to learn to swim for safety purposes. And, she thought that swimming would give Michael yet another outlet for his energy. She also hoped it would help take his mind off his father's absence.

Afraid of the Water

Despite the fact that he would become one of the greatest swimmers in history, Michael did not like swimming at first. In fact, he was afraid of the water. He was frightened of sinking and hated getting his face wet. He begged to be allowed out of the pool. But his mother insisted he learn to swim, and Cathy Lears, his instructor, turned a deaf ear to his pleas. Phelps describes what happened:

> You would think that on the first day I hit the water I just sort of turned into a dolphin and never wanted to leave the pool. No way, I hated it. We're talking screaming, kick-

ing, fit-throwing, goggle-tossing hate . . . I may have been the younger brother of two great swimmers but as soon as I got in the pool, with Miss Cathy guiding me along, I realized I was scared to get my face wet. We tried it a few times with Miss Cathy holding on to me, but I just didn't feel comfortable. In the shallow end, I was okay, because I realized that if I had to, I could simply stand up on the bottom and not worry about sinking. But when I knew I couldn't stand, I started getting tense, becoming more rigid, less buoyant, unable to swim. Miss Cathy sensed my nervousness, but she also wanted to make sure I kept going and she didn't let me make excuses.[19]

Since Michael was afraid to put his face in the water, Lears taught him to float on his back. That way, he could keep his face dry. And he could not see how deep the water was, so he was less

When he first started swimming, Michael Phelps did not like the water on his face, so his instructor taught him to float on his back like this child.

afraid of sinking. After a few sessions, he started moving his arms and legs and was soon doing the backstroke. After a while he felt confident enough to put his face in the water. Lears taught him to do the Australian crawl (the stroke commonly called freestyle). Before he knew it, Michael was having fun.

A Safe Haven

Once Michael learned to swim, he fell in love with the sport. He felt different in the water—calmer, happier, and more in control. The structure of swimming laps and the boundaries of the lane lines kept him focused. According to his mother, "The pool was really good for Michael. It's a huge rectangle with boundaries. In a pool, there are only so many places you can go. Just back and forth, back and forth. So, he was within his element, within his comfort zone."[20]

Phelps agrees:

What I discovered soon after starting to swim was that the pool was a safe haven. I certainly could not have put that into words then, but can look back and see it now. Two walls at either end. Lane lines on either side. A black stripe on the bottom for direction. I could go fast in the pool, it turned out, in part because being in the pool slowed down my mind. In the water, I felt, for the first time, in control. Swimmers like to say they can 'feel' the water. Even early on I felt it. I didn't have to fight the water. Instead I could feel how I moved in it. How to be balanced. What might make me go faster or slower.[21]

Besides calming him and helping him focus, competing against other swimmers let Michael burn up energy and was an excellent outlet for his competitive nature. Because he progressed rapidly, he found himself swimming with older children. This made him feel important.

In the pool Michael stood out only because of his talent. He was no longer the uncool kid trying to sit in the back of the school bus, or the student who could not focus his attention. His swim cap covered his large ears. His body shape, which made him appear awkward on land, was perfect for moving through water.

The Language of Swimming

The sport of swimming has a language all its own. Here are some common swimming terms.

anchor: the final swimmer in a relay

blocks: the starting platforms, located in front of each lane

club teams: year-round swim teams that are usually divided by age

competitive strokes: the backstroke, breaststroke, butterfly (fly), and freestyle (free)

event: a swim race

finals: championship event in which the winners of the preliminaries (prelims) swim

individual medley (IM): a swimming event in which each of the four swimmers uses a different one of the four competitive strokes

lane: a specific area in which a swimmer is assigned to swim

lane lines: floating dividers between swim lanes

lap: one complete length of the pool

leg: the part of a relay that is swum by an individual swimmer

length: the distance from one end of the pool to the other, or one lap

meet: a complete series of swim events

prelims: races in which swimmers qualify for the finals, also called heats, trials, semi-finals, or preliminaries

qualifying time: set time needed to enter a swim meet

relay: a swimming event in which a team of four swimmers each swims one of the four competitive strokes

While he was swimming, his problems at home and at school seemed to disappear. "I'm just different in the water," he explains. "I just feel at home in it. I work with autistic kids a little, and there's this one kid, once he gets in the water, he's relaxed. He gets happy. That's how I am."[22]

The pool became a refuge for Michael. And swimming became his passion. In the water he found the focus, positive outlet for his energy, and acceptance that he needed.

Chapter 2

"When the Student Is Ready, the Teacher Appears"

When Michael was nine years old, he began training at the North Baltimore Aquatic Club (NBAC) where both his sisters trained. He was the fastest member of his swim group. He was also the youngest—most of the other swimmers were at least two years older than he. Besides being young, Michael was immature for his age. According to his mother, "He would beat everybody by several body lengths, get out of the pool, and then I'd see him making silly faces. He was still a silly little kid."[23]

The group's coach was an easygoing man named Tom Himes. He wanted his swimmers to have fun while they learned the basics of competitive swimming. So he rarely scolded them, even when they misbehaved.

Michael misbehaved often. If he got tired of waiting his turn at swim meets, he jumped into the pool, which disrupted whatever race was in progress. When he lost a race, he got angry. During practice, if he did not want to do something he cried or had a tantrum.

Even when he was out of the water, he caused trouble by running around the pool deck and bothering the other children. "I was a pool rat, running around, sneaking up behind people, stealing their snacks and goggles, tapping them on the shoulder and running away and just causing havoc,"[24] he explains.

Michael gained a reputation as both gifted and unruly. Although he was already amassing a collection of trophies and medals, unless he gained more self-discipline, it was unlikely he would ever reach

Michael Phelps talks to North Baltimore Aquatic Club youth coach Tom Himes on December 11, 2009. Himes coached Phelps from the ages of nine to eleven.

his true potential as a swimmer. It was not until Michael started training under Coach Bob Bowman that he came into his own.

"There is a saying that when the student is ready, the teacher appears," Debbie Phelps says. "No doubt, Bob Bowman was the teacher who appeared just when Michael was ready—on May 5, 1997, a month before Michael's twelfth birthday."[25]

A Bad First Impression

Despite Michael's lack of self-control, he quickly moved up to the advanced swimming group. At age eleven, he was training with thirteen- and fourteen-year-old swimmers. One day after practice, some of Michael's teammates started throwing wet towels and swimsuits around the locker room. When Michael came in to change, the mess was already made, and the boys were laughing and screaming. Hearing the ruckus, Bob Bowman, who had recently joined NBAC's coaching staff, went into the locker room to see what was going on. Hearing Bowman's approaching footsteps, all the boys except Michael, who was not yet dressed, fled through a side door.

Although Bowman and Michael had not yet met, Bowman had heard about Michael and the trouble he caused. Bowman assumed that Michael was behind the mess. He yelled at the boy, demanding to know what Michael had done. Michael yelled back that he had done nothing. Bowman did not believe him, but had no proof to the contrary. So Michael was not punished. But Michael's first impression of the new coach was not a good one. Bowman, too, was unimpressed with Michael. Journalist Amy Shipley, who talked to both men about their first meeting, reports: "As Bowman left the locker room, he thought: 'Thank God I'm never going to have to coach this kid.' Phelps had a similar reaction. 'I don't want to swim for a guy like that,'"[26] he thought.

A New Coach

Much to Michael's and Coach Bob's dismay, they would be working together. Not long after their first encounter, Bowman became the advanced swimming coach. Bowman was well qualified for the job. As a young man, he had swum for Florida State University. After he graduated, he spent the next nine years coaching seven different club swim teams. Many of his swimmers reached the national level, and his teams became well known in the swimming world. None of this increased his appeal to Michael.

If anything, Bowman intimidated Michael. From the start the coach was wise to Michael's tricks and let Michael know it. "I couldn't put anything past him," Phelps says. "If he told twenty of us to swim ten laps at different intervals and I only swam nine, he called me on it. If he asked us to show up at the top of the hour and I arrived at 5:01, he'd be at the front door to ask why. If I splashed a teammate when he wasn't looking, those eyes in the back of Bob's head would let him know, and he would be sure to let me know that he knew. Bob scared me."[27]

A Strict Disciplinarian

Bowman did not think he would be working with Michael for very long. He planned to stay at the NBAC only long enough to earn enough money to pay for graduate school, where he intended to study music. But while he was at the club, he expected all his swimmers, including Michael, to behave.

Michael's tears and tantrums did not move the coach. He disciplined the boy when he did not do what he was supposed to do.

Bob Bowman coaches Michael Phelps in Melbourne, Australia, at the World Championships on March 23, 2007. Phelps was intimidated by Bowman when they first began working together.

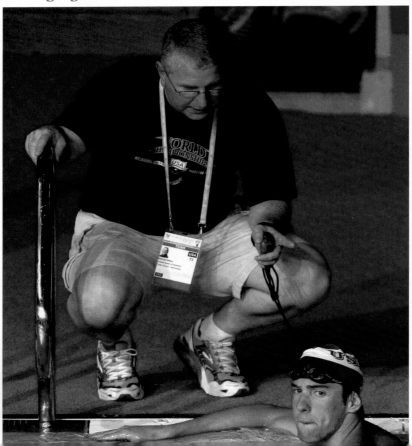

Plus, Bowman was a stern taskmaster and a perfectionist. He worked hard and always did his best. He expected his swimmers to do the same. Phelps has compared him to a marine drill sergeant.

Early on, he and Michael had a serious run in. Bowman instructed the advanced swimmers to swim 200 meters (219 yds.) at racing speed. Everyone but Michael obeyed. He purposefully swam slowly. When the swimmers got out of the pool, Bowman ordered Michael to get back in the water and do what he had been told to do. Michael refused. "I uncorked one of the great twelve-year-old tantrums of all time," Phelps says. "I screamed, 'you can't make me do it.' And so on. A huge, horrible public scene, a direct challenge to Bob's authority in front of everyone. Bob said to me, you can do what you want, but as of now you're not a member of NBAC, and until you come back and do the set, you never will be."[28]

Michael went home in tears. His mother called Bowman. The coach arranged to meet with her and Michael early the next morning. When Debbie Phelps heard what had happened, she supported Bowman. At that point Michael realized that, if he wanted to continue swimming, he would have to obey the coach. Michael loved to swim. The very thought of giving it up horrified him. So, he got into the pool and swam as fast as he could. He did not stop until Bowman was satisfied. "If it sounds now like Bob was a trainer, breaking the wild horse that was me," Phelps says, "well, it is what it is."[29]

Coach and Psychologist

Threatening to throw Michael out of the pool was only one method Bowman used to change Michael's behavior. Bowman had a bachelor's degree in psychology. He made a point of getting to know his swimmers and learning what made them tick. He understood that Michael's love of winning drove him. He used the boy's competitive nature to motivate him. He challenged Michael to compete, not only against other swimmers, but against himself—better his own time, break his own records, improve his strokes. The concept was new to Michael, but he embraced it. Soon, instead of creating mischief, Michael was focused on watching the clock and estimating split times, that is, how fast he had to swim in the first half of a race to complete the race in a specific time. "With Bob's prompting," he explains, "I discovered something else about myself early on, too. I could be motivated not just by winning. By improving my strokes. Hitting split times. Setting records. Doing my best times. There was any number of things I could do to get better. Winning never gets old, but there was a way to win that showed I was getting better, and could get better still."[30]

Another way Bowman motivated Michael was by challenging him to do difficult things. For instance, when Bowman first started working with Michael, the boy used a two-beat kick while swimming freestyle. That means he did two kicks for every stroke cycle. Bowman wanted him to switch to a six-beat kick, which is more difficult but helps a swimmer go faster.

Michael was resistant. The six-beat kick was hard. He had been winning races with the two-beat kick and was comfortable with it. Bowman used reverse psychology on Michael to get him to switch to the more difficult kick. He told Michael that he was not mature enough to go through a whole day using a six-beat kick. That got Michael's competitive juices flowing. He had to prove Bowman wrong, which was what the coach was counting on.

He used the same technique to get Michael to swim faster or train longer. In later years he gave Michael newspaper articles that predicted Michael would lose a race, knowing that seeing the articles would motivate him to prove the writer wrong. Phelps readily admits: "If someone says I can't, then it makes me all the more determined to prove that I can."[31]

At other times, Bowman motivated Michael by assuring the boy that he was confident Michael could do something, even if it was something that seemed impossible. Michael rarely had teachers who told him he could achieve. The experience of having someone other than his mother believe in him made Michael start to believe in himself. And it inspired him to work harder. According to Phelps, "Bob has, without question, helped refine my intense drive and dedication. He has also, without question, helped me believe that anything is possible. Two seconds faster than the world record? Doesn't matter. Three seconds faster? Doesn't matter. You can swim as fast as you want. You can do anything you want."[32]

Bob Bowman, swimming coach for Michael Phelps, has coached him since age eleven and helped him to redirect his negative emotions.

Bowman also helped Michael to redirect his negative emotions. When Michael got angry because he lost a race or did not beat his own personal record, Bowman told him to use that anger to swim harder in his next race. Pretty soon, instead of throwing his goggles or having a tantrum, Michael used that energy to swim faster.

Bowman understood Michael. He knew which buttons to push to motivate the boy. At the same time, by consistently challenging Michael and helping him gain more self-control, Bowman helped build Michael's self-confidence. Each time Michael succeeded, he felt better and better about himself. Bowman, according to Debbie Phelps, made Michael "believe that no matter what

he set out to accomplish, it was possible. . . . He coached the total swimmer—the total human being."[33]

Lots of Talent

It did not take Bowman long to realize that Michael had the mak-
ings of a champion. He was fast. He had endless energy. He loved
to swim. And he had the perfect body shape for a swimmer. But
a lot of children had potential. It would take a lot of hard work,

History of the Olympics

The first written record of the Olympics dates back to 776
B.C. in ancient Greece. The only sport in the first Olympics
was a 192-meter (210-yard) run. The Olympics were held
every four years until A.D. 393, when Roman emperor Theo-
dosius I, banned them. Chariot racing, boxing, horseracing,
and marathon running had been added to the events by that
time.

The Olympics were not revived until 1896. The 1896
Olympics were held in Athens, Greece. In this Olympics 300
athletes from 13 countries participated. In comparison,
10,500 athletes from 205 countries participated in the 2008
Olympics.

Events in the 1896 Olympics included swimming, pole
vaulting, weight lifting, cycling, running, target shooting,
gymnastics, and tennis. Swimming was held in the Aegean
Sea, where athletes had to contend with huge waves and
cold water.

The Olympics were held every four years, except in 1916,
1940, and 1944 due to World Wars I and II. Women first participated in the Olympics in 1900.

The Winter Olympics began in 1924. Events included ski-
ing, ice skating, bobsledding, tobogganing, and ice hockey.
They were held in the same year as the Summer Olympics
until 1992 when they began being held two years apart from
the Summer Olympics.

sacrifice, and dedication for the boy to reach his potential. Swimming had to become the primary focus of his life. At the time Michael was playing lacrosse, baseball, and soccer, and he was swimming. Sometimes he would go from a game to the pool to another game. He loved playing all these sports. But Michael would have to drop his other sports if he wanted to be a world champion swimmer or an Olympic-level swimmer. He would have to spend all his free time swimming, which meant he would have almost no social life outside of the pool.

Bowman talked to Debbie Phelps about Michael's talent. According to his predictions, if Michael dedicated himself to swimming and he continued progressing at his current rate, he would be ready for the Olympics by 2004. By 2012, Bowman believed, Michael would make Olympic history.

Dedication and Challenges

The type of dedication necessary to reach this goal was not new to the Phelps family. Whitney Phelps had made it to the 1996 Olympic trials. A back injury ruined her Olympic dreams. The experience had been heartbreaking. Debbie Phelps did not know whether she wanted to relive the experience with Michael. But she trusted Bowman. According to Debbie, he promised her that he would "take it one step at a time, building the skills, planting the seeds, laying the foundation. The only thing he warned of is that if we weren't careful, if we either pushed too hard or didn't give Michael the challenges he needed, as well as the opportunity to be a kid, it could all go the other way."[34]

Bowman did challenge Michael. He told the boy that if he gave up his other sports and devoted himself to swimming, there was a possibility he could make the Olympics in 2000. Although this date was earlier than Bowman planned, he used it as a way to gain Michael's interest. It worked. According to Phelps, "He said to me . . . that if I wanted to make the Olympic team . . . in 2000, I could as a 15 year old. And I was like, 'Okay, that sounds kind of cool—all right . . . I'll stop all my other sports, focus on swimming, and see if I can make the Olympic team. . . .' And sure enough . . . I made my first Olympic team. . . . And then six

Michael Phelps's sister, Whitney Phelps, rests during the Pan Pacific Games in Atlanta, Georgia, in August 1995. Although she made it to the 1996 Olympic trials, a back injury kept her from the Olympics.

months later after that I broke my first world record, and I knew right then that something special was going to happen."[35] So did Bowman. He gave up his plans to study music and dedicated himself to coaching Phelps.

Conflict and Respect

As Michael got to know Bowman better, the coach no longer intimidated him. But it was not always smooth sailing. They both were stubborn and frequently disagreed. Their poolside shouting matches became legendary in the swimming world. "Bob rides Michael pretty hard," Eddie Reese, the men's head coach of USA Swimming, admits. "But it's all in Michael's interest. Maybe it's not what's best for him in that moment, but Bob can see down the line. If you've got children and you want to take good care of them, it doesn't mean you let them do everything they want to do. You've got to put you're foot down sometimes."[36]

Nor was Michael easy to coach. He had a mind of his own, and he knew just what to say and do to rile up Bowman. Occasionally, he would pick a fight with the coach just because he could. "Sometimes I wish he didn't know me so well," Bowman admits, "because he can push my buttons like no other and vice versa, right? But we're so close right now that we communicate on a level that the typical coach and athlete cannot. I can watch him swim in warm-ups, know what he's doing, give him a hand signal, and he knows what I'm saying."[37]

Their closeness developed over time. Even when the two argue, underneath there is mutual respect and affection. And their fights, which still occur occasionally, never last long. According to Bowman, "Both of us are brutally honest with each other all the time. That's why we get in some heated things, because a lot of times people don't want to hear the truth. Whenever we have our things, we vent, and then it is over."[38]

USA Swimming

USA Swimming is the governing group for swim clubs and the sport of swimming in the United States. It establishes the rules for swimming events and for what constitutes proper behavior for swimmers. It sponsors swim meets, including swim meets for swimmers with disabilities, swim camps, and training sessions for coaches. The United States Nationals, World Championships, and Olympic teams are selected through USA Swimming-sponsored events.

USA Swimming is also involved in promoting the sport of swimming. Its "Splash Nation" program supports learn-to-swim programs throughout the United States.

USA Swimming has more than three hundred thousand members. They include coaches, volunteers, and swimmers of all ages.

A Complex Relationship

In many ways their relationship is much like that of a father and son. In and out of the pool, Bowman has been a part of many important moments in Michael's life. For instance, when Michael was thirteen he went to his first school dance. Bowman allowed him to leave practice fifteen minutes early so that he could get dressed. But the boy had problems. Growing up in a house filled with women, he had no idea how to tie his tie. Bowman taught him how. Then, he rebuttoned Michael's shirt because the boy had missed a button. "We've had some really fun moments like that, and that's one of the reasons we're still together,"[39] Bowman explains.

Michael Phelps and his coach Bob Bowman joke around during the 2003 ConocoPhilips Swimming Championships at the University of Maryland.

And, like many fathers, Bowman taught Michael how to drive. After Michael got his license, Bowman sometimes lent Michael his car, which had a manual transmission. He was there to rescue the boy when he had driving problems. "I always had trouble getting into first gear, especially on hills," Phelps admits. "I was driving to school one morning and there was this busy intersection in Baltimore and rush hour traffic. I stall in the middle of the hill. . . . It's little things like that Bob is always there for."[40]

Bowman spent holidays and special occasions with the Phelps family. He took Michael on outings to see the thoroughbred racehorses that he raised as a hobby. He reassured Michael and helped him cope when Michael hurt his back in 2004. "He saw something in me," says Phelps, "and really has never given up on me, through good times and bad. He's been able to help me grow from the little 11-year-old swimmer who didn't really know what he was doing to the person I am today."[41] After more than a decade together, neither can imagine his life without the other.

Chapter 3

"The Motivation Machine"

Under Bowman's coaching, Michael was becoming well known in the swimming world. Success did not come without effort. Setting goals and working to achieve them kept Michael motivated and helped him to succeed no matter what challenges he faced.

A Very Difficult Goal

When Michael was in seventh grade, he decided that he no longer wanted to take ADHD medication. He came to think of it as a crutch and believed he could focus without it. His ability to focus in the swimming pool, his increasing skill at controlling and redirecting his frustration and anger, and the self-discipline that Bowman was working hard to instill in him made him believe he could cope without the medication.

Michael told his mother what he wanted to do. She worried about whether he would be able to succeed in school without medication. Michael was confident that if he could focus in the pool, he could focus anywhere. His mother agreed to let him try. She knew that if he failed, he could always go back on the medication.

Over the course of a year, Michael's doctor gradually weaned him off the medication. He went from three doses a day, to two, then to one, and finally to none. Michael utilized the time management skills his mother taught him to keep himself on task, the

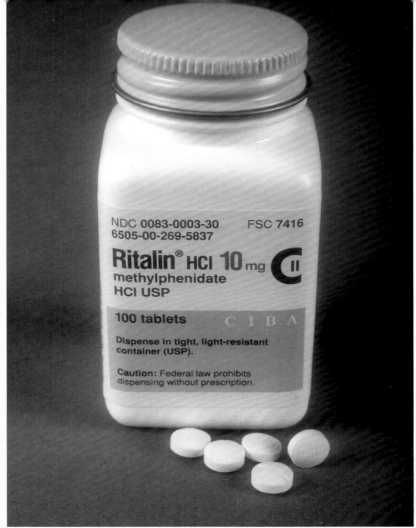

At the age of nine, Michael Phelps was prescribed Ritalin to combat his ADHD, but he was weaned off of it by the time he was twelve.

structure of his training schedule to help him burn off excess energy, and the skills he developed in swimming to keep focused. His mother helped him by hiring tutors, making sure he got special assistance in school, working with him at home, and making the best use of his time.

It was not easy. Michael did not become an A student, but he passed his classes. This was a huge accomplishment. Achieving such a difficult goal boosted Michael's self-confidence. It made him believe that no matter what goal he set, if he worked hard enough, he could accomplish anything. He recalls: "In middle school I said to my mom, 'I don't want to take this anymore, I can do this on my own.' . . . I was confident that I could do it, and once I was able to do that, it was kind of easy from there. . . . I think with swimming, I found something where I can sort of— the aggression that I had, I can take out in the pool. And I learned, as I got older and older, that I can focus on anything I do. . . . I learned from swimming and making the decision to get off Ritalin [ADHD medicine]."[42]

The Goal Sheet

Michael began setting other goals that concerned his performance in the pool. Goal setting was not new to Phelps. His mother encouraged her children to set objectives and to work hard to

Moving Through Water

Physics plays a key role in swimming. Swimmers must contend with three types of resistance, or drag.

Form drag is resistance caused by the swimmer's body. Keeping the body straight and tight with the toes pointed helps lower form drag. To see how strong form drag can be, try moving through water with your arms and legs extended horizontally.

Wave drag is resistance caused when swimmers move the water. The faster people swim, the more waves they create. Swimmers with smoother strokes splash less, thereby minimizing wave drag. Lane ropes help lessen wave drag between swim lanes.

Frictional drag is resistance caused by a swimmer's clothes and body hair. Wearing a swim cap and a form-fitting swimsuit lessens frictional drag.

achieve them. "We had to have goals, drive, and determination," Michael explains. "We were going to strive for excellence and to reach excellence you have to work at it and for it."[43] Bowman, too, encouraged Phelps to aim high.

Michael had set mental goals before. Now he started writing them down. He kept a sheet on which he recorded his swimming ambitions for the upcoming year beside his bed. On it he listed the events he wanted to swim in and the times he wanted to hit in each event. Since he and Bowman were the only people who could do anything about his goals, the coach was the only person Michael shared his sheet with. He never showed it to his mother or his sisters.

Bowman never commented about Michael's aims. He never said an objective was unattainable or not lofty enough. He just looked at the list and then put it away. Nor did Michael or Bowman share Michael's ambitions with the press. The goals have always been a secret between the two.

Moving from One Goal to the Next

Phelps found that having a goal sheet kept him focused. Once he achieved an objective, he checked it off and moved on to the next one on his list. "I start with my first one," he explains, "and once I got that one checked off the goal list it's almost like I just throw it over my shoulder, just put it behind me and move to the next one, and I just keep moving on."[44]

Indeed, he used the same kind of procedure to keep from becoming overwhelmed and losing his focus when he swam in multiple events in the Olympics. He concentrated on his first event, swam it, and then put it behind him. He did not worry about what happened in an event once it was complete, nor did he think about a future event until he reached it. In this manner, he was able to keep all of his attention focused on the task at hand.

Aiming High

Because Michael wanted to swim in multiple events and keep bettering his times, his goals were set very high. Bowman designed Michael's training program to help him reach his aims. It was a

Michael Phelps is known for setting swim-time goals and meeting them.

brutal program, which kept getting tougher. Indeed, by the time Michael was in high school, he was training up to five hours a day. To increase his strength and endurance, he often swam with just one arm and leg, in sneakers, tied to a pulley, with an inner tube around his ankles, or in a weighted vest.

As another tool for reaching his goals, Bowman encouraged Michael to visualize a race in his head as if he were watching a video. "When I'm about to fall asleep, I visualize to the point that I know exactly what I want to do: dive, glide, stroke, flip, reach the wall, hit the split time to the hundredth [of a second], then swim back again for as many times as I need to finish the race. It's pretty vivid,"[45] Phelps explains.

Visualizing in this manner helped him a lot. In fact, during the 2008 Olympics Phelps's goggles filled with water, so he could not see. To keep from crashing into the wall, Phelps counted his strokes. He knew how many strokes he needed per lap because he had counted them repeatedly in his mental video. "I would visualize the best-and-worst-case scenarios. Whether I get disqualified or my goggles fill up with water or I lose my goggles or I come in last, I'm ready for anything,"[46] he says.

Remarkably, in 1998, the first year that Michael kept a goal sheet, he hit all of his targeted times to the tenth of a second. He has continued to do so fairly consistently ever since. For example, in 1999 he set a goal of swimming the 200-meter butterfly in 2:04.68 minutes. He swam the event at the Junior Nationals in exactly that time. According to Bowman, Phelps "is right on the money about where he ends up, almost always. Pretty amazing."[47] Neither Phelps nor Bowman can explain how Phelps does this. Bowman says that this ability is just one of the many things that makes Phelps special.

Working toward his goals motivated Michael. He became, according to Bowman, "the motivation machine. Bad moods, good moods, he channels everything for gain. He is motivated by success, he loves to swim fast and when he does he goes back and trains better. He's motivated by failure, by money, by people saying things about him, just anything that comes along he turns into a reason to train harder, swim better."[48]

An Olympian

Michael's goal setting quickly paid off. By the time he was fourteen, he was featured in *Swim World* magazine. At fifteen he held the American record for his age group in the 100- and 200-meter butterfly, the 400- and 800-meter freestyle, and the 200- and 400-meter individual medley (IM) in which he did all four competitive strokes—freestyle, breast stroke, butterfly, and backstroke. His progress was so far ahead of Bowman's original predictions that there was a chance that Michael would make the 2000 Olympic team, which was one of the teenager's goals.

Michael entered three events in the 2000 Olympic trials, the 200-meter butterfly and the 200- and 400-meter IMs. Only two swimmers per event qualify for the Olympics. Michael had to come in first or second to make the Olympic team. Few people expected that he would do so. He was very young, and he was competing against the best swimmers in the nation, not just in his age group.

He came in eleventh in the 400 IM, swimming well below his personal best. He did not do well in the 200 IM either, but his performance in the 200-meter butterfly stunned the swimming world. At 150 meters he was in fifth place. Then, in the last 50 meters he came racing up from behind and managed to finish in second place. He had won a place on the 2000 Olympic team. "Being an Olympian and representing America was always my goal," he explains. "Going into the 2000 trials, I did not have high expectations; I just wanted to go and have fun and swim my best, and I did, and I made the team."[49]

The Olympics were held in Sydney, Australia. Michael's goal was to win a gold medal there. Instead, he came in fifth in the 200-meter butterfly. He swam the event in 1:56.50 minutes, which was a personal best for him. But he could not check winning an Olympic gold medal off his goal sheet just yet. That made him all the more determined to make it happen in the future. According to Phelps, "Not accomplishing a goal, no matter what it is for me, just makes me want it that much more."[50]

Setting Records

Being an Olympian made Michael a local hero. When he returned from Sydney, he was greeted in the airport by a limousine filled with his friends. The next day his high school held a big celebration. He even got to throw out the first pitch at a Baltimore Orioles game.

Michael did not let his fame go to his head. Not earning a medal in Sydney made him train harder. He set a new goal for himself. He wanted to break the world record in the 200-meter butterfly at the 2001 U.S. Nationals in Austin, Texas, which he did. At fifteen years and nine months old, he became the youngest male swimmer in history to hold a world record. "Not accomplishing my goal in Sydney had driven me for all the months in between,"

Michael Phelps, the youngest male swimmer in history to hold a world record, swims during the men's 200-meter butterfly competition in Sydney, Australia, at the 2000 Olympics.

he explains. "I had always known how badly it hurt to lose, how much I hated it. Now I had concrete proof of how losing could motivate me to reach my goals at the highest levels of swimming."[51]

A few months later, he bettered his time and broke his own world record in the 2001 World Championships in Fukuoka, Japan. Michael had now won his first world title.

That same year, he signed a four-year endorsement contract with Speedo, the swimwear manufacturer. That contract has since been renewed through 2013. In exchange for a large sum of money, including the company's agreeing to pay for Michael's college education, Michael promised to use Speedo products and make personal appearances for the company. He also became an advisor to the company's Aqualab team, which develops new swimming products. At sixteen he was a professional swimmer—the youngest professional male swimmer in the United States. With the money he was making, he bought his mother a Mercedes Benz. It was his way of thanking her for all she had done for him. And, shortly after he got his driver's license, he bought himself a Cadillac Escalade.

New Goals

Michael's success got him thinking about the 2004 Olympics, which were going to be held in Athens, Greece. He set a goal of winning medals in four events, the 100- and 200-meter butterfly and the 200- and 400-meter individual medleys. To help him do this, Bowman had him swimming about 85,000 meters (52.82 miles) per week.

Shave and Taper

Before a major swim meet, swimmers go through a period that is known as "shave and taper." Tapering involves cutting back on training. This allows swimmers' bodies to rest to increase their energy level and maximize their performance. When swimmers taper, they do not stop training entirely. Instead, they train less intensely and rest more.

Timing for tapering is crucial. It varies from swimmer to swimmer. If it is too short, the swimmer may be overtired. If it is too long, the swimmer may be out of shape. It is up to the coach to decide how much tapering a swimmer needs. Tapering may last anywhere from a few days to six weeks. In general, older swimmers, those who are more muscular, and those who swim distance events need longer tapering periods.

Shave happens just before a meet. To help lessen resistance in the water, swimmers shave all their body hair that is not covered by their swimsuit or swim cap.

Michael Phelps (top) and Thomas Malchow swim the 200-meter butterfly in Barcelona, Spain, at the 2003 World Championships. Phelps won the event and secured four gold medals overall.

Michael's ability to achieve his goals was tested at the 2003 World Championships in Barcelona, Spain, where, for the first time in a world swim meet, he swam in multiple events. His performance was stellar. He won six medals, four of which were gold. In doing so, he broke five world records, a first for any swimmer in a world championship. And he broke two of these records in two events on the same day, another swimming first.

The Mark Spitz Challenge

After the 2003 World Championships, the press began comparing Michael to Mark Spitz. Spitz is considered to be one of the greatest swimmers of all times. He won seven Olympic gold medals in the 1972 Olympics in Munich, the most by any swimmer in any one Olympics until 2008.

When Michael qualified for eight events in the 2004 Olympics, Speedo offered to give Michael $1 million if he could equal Spitz's seven gold medal record in Athens. The challenge captured the public's imagination, and all eyes were on Michael.

Michael did well in Athens. Although he did not equal Spitz's record, Phelps turned in an amazing performance. He won six gold medals and two bronze medals.

Wanting a Challenge

One bronze medal was for the 200-meter freestyle. This was Michael's weakest event. Many people said he should not have entered the race. He could have entered the 200-meter backstroke instead, an event for which he held the world record and was favored to win. But he insisted on swimming in the 200-meter freestyle.

He wanted the chance to compete against Australian swimming legend, Ian Thorpe. At the time Thorpe was considered to be Australia's greatest swimmer. Going into the race, Michael knew he had little chance of winning, but he wanted the opportunity to swim against the best. Challenging himself was more important to him than taking home $1 million. He explains: "I wouldn't want to spend my career training every day without measuring myself against the best. That's why I wanted to swim this race. I wanted

Michael Phelps (right) and Ian Thorpe, Australia's swimming legend, at the 2004 Olympic Games in Athens. Phelps's goal was to swim against Thorpe, whom he considered a major challenge.

to leave that pool knowing I had swum my best race against my own expectations and against someone I respect as much as Ian Thorpe. The point of competition isn't always to take the easiest way out, but to meet the biggest challenge."[52]

Loyal Teammate and Good Sport

Michael's other bronze was for the 4x100 freestyle relay, which involved four swimmers each swimming 100 meters freestyle. Each

Michael Phelps congratulates swimming teammates, including Ian Crocker, after receiving the bronze medal for the men's 4 x 100 relay at the 2004 Olympics in Athens.

swimmer depends on the teammates' performances. If one swims badly, it is often impossible for the other swimmers to make up the difference. That is what happened in this race. Michael's teammate, Ian Crocker, was feeling sick and did not swim as well as he could. He fell one body length behind the competition. The other swimmers could not make up the time, so the team came in third.

Michael's final race in Athens was the butterfly leg of the 400-meter medley relay. Medley relay teams consist of four swimmers each of whom swims a different stroke. But there are actually eight swimmers on the relay team. The faster two swimmers in each competitive stroke qualify for the event. The fastest swims in the finals, while the other swims in the semifinal race. Going into the Olympics, Ian Crocker, the 100-meter-butterfly world-record holder, was expected to swim in the final. So Michael, with the second fastest butterfly time, swam in the semifinal. When Michael upset Crocker in the individual 100-meter butterfly to win a gold medal, he earned the right to replace Crocker in the final relay.

The 400-medley relay was the last swimming event in the Olympics. Crocker, a gold medalist in the 2000 Olympics, had been ill early in the Athens games and had not won a gold medal. Now he was feeling better. Michael decided to relinquish his place in the final relay to Crocker so that Crocker would have a final chance to win a gold medal. If the final team medaled, they and the semifinal team would be awarded medals. If Crocker swam poorly, Michael would lose his chance for a sixth gold medal. Michael was willing to take the chance. "Ian deserved to swim that race,"[53] he insists.

It was a very kind and sportsmanlike act on Michael's part. According to author Bob Schaller, "Phelps' act of giving up that relay spot to a teammate was arguably the most memorable and talked-about moment of the games. Phelps . . . showed a level of class and consideration for his teammates that set him apart. With the 400-medley relay as the last swimming event of the Olympics, Phelps was remembered with respect, even as he looked forward to four years from that point."[54]

Crocker swam well, and the relay team earned a gold medal. By winning six gold and two bronze medals, Michael had become the second athlete in history to win a total of eight medals at any one Olympics. In 1980 Soviet gymnast Alexander Ditiatin was the first. Michael left Athens feeling proud of his achievement. Yet, because he had not matched Spitz's record of seven gold medals, some people called him a failure. In the coming years, they would be forced to eat their words.

Chapter 4

Ups and Downs

Even though Phelps had not matched Spitz's gold medal record, his performance in Athens made him a celebrity. He made many public appearances, was featured on the covers of magazines such as *Sports Illustrated* and *Men's Journal*, and appeared on a number of television shows. He also gained many lucrative endorsement deals. At nineteen years old, he was earning more than $5 million a year.

Despite his wealth and stardom, Phelps's primary focus was preparing for the 2008 Olympics in Beijing. "I didn't yet know how good I could be. There was obviously more to do to get me to deliver my best. . . . I fully expected to get better,"[55] he explains. He had three big swim meets, the 2005 World Championships in Montreal, the 2006 Pan Pacifics in Victoria, Canada, and the 2007 World Championships in Melbourne, Australia, to test himself. His performance in them would measure his progress and readiness for the Olympics.

A lot happened before Phelps headed to Beijing. No matter what occurred, he kept focused on his goals. And, he was quick to take responsibility for all his actions, whether good or bad.

Back Problems

After the 2004 Olympics, Phelps went on a tour with his teammates Ian Crocker and Lenny Krayzelburg. They visited schools and pools across the United States where they gave swimming lessons and

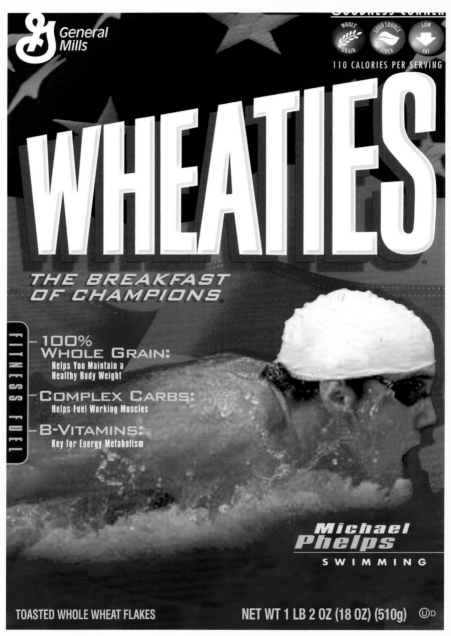

After his stellar performance at the 2004 Olympics in Athens, Michael Phelps was honored by having his image on a box of Wheaties cereal.

demonstrations to children. During the tour, Phelps's back hurt. Years earlier a back injury had ended Whitney Phelps's Olympic hopes. Having witnessed what a back injury did to his sister, Phelps was especially fearful about the same thing happening to him.

His fears were grounded. Repeatedly stretching his spine, gave him a stress fracture, a tiny crack in his backbone. To help it heal, he had to wear a removable back brace and stay out of the pool for six weeks. If this did not work, he would have to get surgery. Although everyone was hopeful Phelps's back would heal, he could not keep from worrying. He explains: "I tried not to think that my career might end prematurely, as hers [Whitney's] did, but of course it entered my mind."[56]

A Terrible Choice

Without his rigid training schedule, Phelps's life lacked the structure he needed. He found himself at loose ends, worried about his future, and full of pent-up energy. On November 4, 2004, he attended a party where beer was served.

Phelps never drank alcohol in high school, although some of his classmates did. He had a celebratory alcoholic drink after the

After drinking three bottles of beer, Olympic swimmer Michael Phelps drove through a stop sign and was arrested for driving under the influence in November 2004.

Olympics in Athens where the legal drinking age is eighteen. Other than that, he rarely, if ever, drank alcohol. But on this occasion, he had three beers, which put his blood alcohol level right above the legal limit for driving. Moreover, he was nineteen years old, two years under the legal drinking age in Maryland.

When it came time to leave the party, he asked a friend to drive him home. But after a group of other partygoers made negative comments about Phelps handing his keys over to another driver, Phelps, who could not resist a challenge, decided to drive. A state trooper pulled him over because he had driven through a stop sign. His blood alcohol tested just above the legal limit. He was arrested and charged with driving under the influence of alcohol, driving while impaired, underage drinking, and failure to obey a stop sign.

Taking Responsibility for His Actions

Phelps felt awful about what he had done. He knew he had messed up, and immediately took responsibility for his actions. He called Bowman and his press agent, Peter Carlisle, to confess what happened. Telling Bowman was difficult. He expected the coach to come down hard on him, which he did. But Bowman was also supportive. He understood that Phelps was still a teenager and apt to make bad choices and mistakes. "Michael feels like he let everyone down who supported him and he has, clearly," Bowman told reporters. "When you see Michael swimming, he just seems superhuman. You forget that he's 19 and he's just trying to grow up."[57]

It was even harder for Phelps to tell his mother what happened. He knew this incident could ruin his career, but his biggest concern was how his actions would disappoint and hurt her. "I had let down my mom. Other people around me, good people, knew me as a swimmer. She was the person who would always look at me as her son, regardless of whether I ever jumped into a pool again. She didn't care about raising a gold medalist, she wanted to raise a son who did the right thing. . . . I had let her down. . . . Of course, she was forgiving and understanding, but she was also hurt. . . . I hated putting her in that position."[58]

Once he spoke to his mother, Phelps contacted the media. He wanted to own up to his mistake and let his fans know how sorry he was. "I made a mistake," he told members of the Associated Press. "I wanted to share my feelings and I know that getting in

Michael Phelps speaks to reporters after pleading guilty to drunk driving charges. He was fined and given probation on December 29, 2004.

a car with anything to drink is wrong, dangerous and is unacceptable. I'm 19, but I was taught that no matter how old you are, you should always take responsibility for your actions, which I will do. I'm very sorry it happened."[59]

Probation

Phelps pleaded guilty at his trial. He faced up to a year in prison. However, since he had never been in trouble before and took responsibility for his actions, instead of imprisoning him the judge fined Phelps $350, put him on probation, and ordered him to

Working with Kids

Michael Phelps likes working with kids. He frequently visits the local Boys and Girls Club in Aberdeen, Maryland, where he signs autographs, talks to, and plays basketball with the children.

He especially likes working with children with special needs. In 2002 he befriended seven-year-old Stevie Hansen, a promising swimmer facing brain tumor surgery, who trained at NBAC. Michael visited Stevie before he went to the hospital. While Stevie was in the hospital, Phelps sent him balloons and baskets of candy. Phelps attended one of Stevie's swim meets. And before the boy died in 2007, Phelps sat at his bedside holding his hand. Phelps considers Hansen one of his heroes because of the boy's courage.

Mason Sourhoff, an autistic teenager, is another young swimmer Phelps has taken under his wing. Phelps clowns around with him at the pool. According to Mason's mother, Mason's "speech, his actions, they're very different and a lot of people don't know how to react. Michael could care less about all that. He has such a young spirit, and there is a goofiness about him that is so attractive to kids."

Quoted in Alan Shipnuck, "Sportsman of the Year," *Sports Illustrated*, December 8, 2008, p. 44.

perform community service. If he satisfactorily completed his community service, his criminal record would be erased.

Phelps put in more hours of community service than the court required. He talked to young people about the dangers of drinking and driving, and about making good choices. He wanted to prevent them from doing what he had done. "I learned from this mistake," he says, "and will continue learning from this mistake for the rest of my life."[60]

Following Bob

Around this time, Bob Bowman was offered a job coaching in Ann Arbor, Michigan. There he would coach at the University of Michigan and at Club Wolverine, a swim club noted for its world-class swimmers, which uses the pool at the University of Michigan. The job was an excellent opportunity for Bowman. But he did not want to leave Phelps. When Phelps heard about the offer, he did not hesitate. He did not want Bowman to give up such a good chance. He pledged to go to Michigan, too, where he would train with Bowman at Club Wolverine. While he was there, he planned to take classes at the University of Michigan. He was confident the university would allow him to enroll because of his swimming talent, which it did. "No other coach could have gotten me as far as Bob," Phelps explains. "I like Ann Arbor and I admire Michigan's tradition, but if Bob had accepted a job in Siberia, my decision would have been the same."[61]

When Phelps first arrived in Michigan, he stayed with Bowman. The two were not cut out to be roommates. Bowman treated Phelps more like his son than an equal. He was constantly checking on Phelps, which made Phelps feel like a child. And, because Phelps was living in Bowman's house, Bowman chose what they watched on television and what music they listened to. The two had very different tastes. After a month, Phelps bought a condo in Ann Arbor and moved out.

For the first time in his life, he was on his own. Before going to Michigan, he had depended upon his mother and sisters to take care of him. Now he had to learn to cook, do laundry, clean house, and generally fend for himself. It was a big adjustment.

He made lots of mistakes. His cooking, which he admits tasted a lot like shoe leather, repeatedly set off the smoke detector. He put liquid hand soap into the dishwasher and filled his kitchen with bubbles. But little by little he learned how to take care of himself. According to Hilary Phelps, "I think it helped Michael to learn responsibility. He's a very responsible person in general, but moving away from home taught him how to take care of himself. If he was out of milk, he had to go and buy some more. We are a very protective family, and very protective of Michael, but I think this helped him develop into his own person."[62]

Once he adjusted to being on his own, Phelps liked it. He took a few classes in sports management and business administration, but he did not pursue a degree. His main concern was swimming. He had come to Michigan to train at Club Wolverine under Bowman. He could not swim on the university's team because professional swimmers are not allowed to swim on collegiate teams. Olympians such as Eric Vendt, Chris Thompson, Peter Vanderkaay, and Klete Keller were also training at Club Wolverine. Once Phelps was able to get back in the pool, he enjoyed the camaraderie and the challenge of training with other elite swimmers.

Michael Phelps (left) poses with Peter Vanderkaay and Klete Keller of Club Wolverine at the ConocoPhilips National Championships in August 2005, in Irvine, California.

Bad Times

Unfortunately, Phelps's back problems did not completely go away. He worked with a physical therapist to help strengthen his back. Concerned about Phelps's back, Bowman did not push him hard.

Despite the fact that he had been training less strenuously, Phelps decided to add two new events, the 100- and 400-meter freestyle, to his swimming program. The challenge of competing in new events and not training at 100 percent took its toll on him. Phelps's performance in the 2005 World Championships was not as good as he had hoped. When he entered the semifinal race for the 400-meter freestyle, for the first time since he had started swimming competitively, he failed to make the final of an individual race. A day later he came in seventh in the 100-meter freestyle final. Although he wound up winning five gold medals at the meet, Phelps did not hit most of his goal times or break his personal records. "It was a wake-up call, a slap in the face. I had a lot of work to do. . . . I honestly felt that after setting records every year, I had practically stood still for 12 months,"[63] he says. His lackluster performance at the World Championships spurred Phelps to train harder. "I don't like to lose," he says. "If I fail, I ask myself, 'What can I do to make sure that doesn't happen again?'"[64]

But training harder did not go as well as he hoped. For eighteen months following the 2004 Olympics, he did not break a world record or set a personal best. His personal life, too, was not rosy. His grandmother, whom Phelps was very close to, died. Her death hit him hard. She had taught Phelps how to play poker, one of his favorite pastimes. Throughout his life, they had played cards whenever they got together. Both were highly competitive. Their games were both intense and fun. Phelps missed her companionship and her support.

Phelps spoke at his grandmother's memorial service and gave the funeral director a playing card from a deck the two often used and a pair of his swim goggles to be buried with her. Then he vowed that he would break a new world record in her honor.

Before Phelps could do that, however, he broke the bone beneath his pinky finger of his right hand. Surgery, which involved inserting a titanium plate and three screws into his hand, mended the break. He had to stay out of the pool for three weeks while it healed. During this time he trained by riding a stationary bike.

"If I Want Something Bad Enough"

Phelps began to wonder if his best swimming days were behind him. But he had too many unachieved goals to give up. He believed that if he trained hard enough and kept focused on his goals, things would turn around. "When I am focused, there is not one single thing, person, anything that can stand in my way of doing something. There is not. Never has been. If I want something bad enough, then I'm gonna get there. That's just how I always have been. If I don't get there, watch out—because it's going to be even worse and I'm going to have my head on even tighter and you will not get in my way,"[65] he says.

He did get there. Phelps set three world records at the 2006 Pan Pacific swim meet. He went back to Michigan feeling as if a weight had been lifted from his shoulders. But that did not mean he could sit back and rest on his laurels. He knew that he would have to train even harder if he wanted to medal in multiple events in the 2008 Olympics.

Phelps did not mind working hard. According to him, "When I'm training the best, I'm happy. I'm smiling at workouts, I'm joking around, I'm talking. For the most part throughout my career, I'm happy going in the pool."[66]

Good News

Adding to his happiness, after years of wanting a dog, he got an English bulldog named Herman. Then in March 2007, his sister Whitney gave birth to a baby girl, and Phelps became a doting uncle. And his mother became a middle school principal. She had worked hard for years to reach this goal. Phelps was proud and happy for her. Things were finally looking up.

He headed into the 2007 World Championships with high hopes and lofty goals, all of which he achieved. Phelps won seven gold medals in Melbourne and broke five world records, most by large margins. One of these records was for the 200-meter freestyle, which he swam 1.34 seconds faster than his personal best. In so doing, he beat Ian Thorpe's world record by .20 seconds. This victory was especially sweet for Phelps because before the meet Australian swim coach, Dan Talbot, told the media that Phelps would never beat or even match Thorpe's record. Talbot went on to belittle Phelps's fame and ability.

Talbot's words angered Phelps. But he did not respond verbally. He let his performance in the pool speak for him. The results were so extraordinary that, although Talbot had no response to Phelps's

Michael Phelps (left) and Pieter Van den Hoogenband (of the Netherlands) start the men's 200-meter freestyle at the World Championships in Melbourne. Phelps won the race for the gold and broke a world record with a time of 1:43.86.

Phelps's Prerace Routine

Michael Phelps is known for his focus and determination in the pool. His prerace routine helps him to concentrate. Before a race, he swims warm-up laps, then he changes into a dry swimsuit, puts on his headphones, and listens to hip-hop music for the entire time before the race begins. This helps him to remain calm and focus on his goals. Although he is a fun-loving guy, he sits alone. He does not talk to the other swimmers.

Once he is on the blocks, he does not think about anything. He does not pay attention to the audience or to what the other swimmers are doing. When the race begins, all he thinks about is swimming as fast as he can.

performance, Australian swimmer Grant Hackett told the media: "He is just superhuman. We won't see anything like this again."[67]

A Broken Wrist

With the World Championships over, Phelps focused on the 2008 Olympics. He followed a grueling training schedule that involved hours and hours of full-out racing. He had stopped taking classes, so that his life could completely revolve around his workouts. He ate breakfast, lifted weights, trained on a stationary bike, swam, ate lunch, napped, then returned to the pool where he trained into the night. With each passing day, he was getting faster and stronger.

Then, in October 2007, seven months before the Olympic trials and nine months before the Olympics, he slipped on a patch of ice while getting into his car and broke his right wrist. If it did not heal fast enough, Phelps's Olympic dreams and possibly his whole swimming career would be over. The thought made him cry. He could not let this happen.

At the hospital the doctor offered Phelps two options for treating his hand. The first was putting it in a cast for six weeks. Or, he could surgically repair the bone with a pin, which would take ten days to heal. Phelps did not have to think twice. He chose surgery.

After the surgery Phelps wanted to leave the hospital right away so that he could resume his training. The doctor, however, had other ideas. He said that Phelps could not leave until his heart rate returned to its normal resting rate. As a world-class athlete, Phelps knew how to control his breathing and his heart rate. According to his mother, "Michael leaned back and closed his eyes as he inhaled oxygen as he might use to swim the length of a pool underwater, then he slowly exhaled. . . . It was amazing to watch. . . . After what seemed to be a matter of a few minutes, Michael's heart rate came down to normal levels. The doctors came in and were rather startled but happily gave Michael his walking papers."[68]

Phelps was able to get back in the pool right away. He wore a plastic bag on his hand and trained with a kickboard. Initially, he was depressed. But he put himself in Bowman's capable hands and visualized the best would happen. As it turned out, the extra legwork made his kick and his turns more powerful, which helped him in the Olympics. Talking about the experience, Phelps explains: "It made me realize that things can change in the blink of an eye and it also made me realize that when you use your imagination anything can happen. I was very negative for the first few days after I found out my wrist was broken, and I had a lot of time to think. I realized that all the people that told me I can't do it, that this is going to make it even harder. You know what? I'm gonna do it."[69]

By June, when the Olympic trials rolled around, Phelps had done it. He won all five of his individual events, broke two world records, and earned the right to swim in a total of eight events at the Olympics. August could not arrive soon enough for him.

Chapter 5

Changing Swimming Forever

Phelps had two goals for the 2008 Olympics. The first was to do something no one else had ever done, win eight gold medals in a single Olympics. The second was to get the American public as excited about swimming as they were about sports like baseball and football.

Phelps first came up with his second goal during the 2000 Olympics in Australia. There, swimming is a very popular spectator sport. Phelps wanted to see swimming elevated to the same level in the United States. Since then, he had been working to make this happen. In 2004 when he tried to match Mark Spitz's gold medal record, he hoped that the publicity surrounding the million-dollar challenge would raise the public's interest in swimming. Now, he had high hopes that by winning eight gold medals in Beijing he would spark even more enthusiasm for the sport. He explains: "I don't want this sport to be an every-four-years-sport. In between the four years, there's really not as much exposure as I'd like. . . . My whole goal is to change the sport of swimming in a positive way. I think it can go even farther. That's where I hope to take it."[70]

Against the Odds

Phelps knew that he had to win each race to hold the public's interest. This would be very difficult. Over the course of nine days, he would be swimming in seventeen races counting semifinal and final events. Some of these were back-to-back. It would take

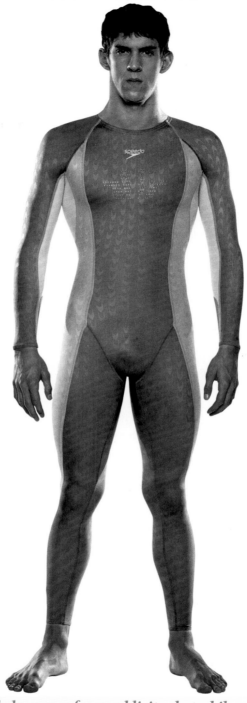

Michael Phelps poses for a publicity shot while wearing Speedo's Fastskin FSII performance suit.

High-Tech Swimsuits

Competitive swimsuits are made to facilitate fast swimming. Over the years, changes in swimsuits have made them more effective. In 1974 Lycra was introduced. The synthetic fabric made swimsuits fit tighter, which lessened drag. In 2000 a new fabric called Fastskin was developed. Its texture and smoothness was modeled after a shark's skin. Suits made of Fastskin reduced drag by up to 4 percent.

Using technology developed by the National Aeronautics and Space Administration, in 2008 lighter weight suits that incorporated polyurethane, a rubberlike substance, in the panels became popular. They made swimmers more buoyant, which allowed them to go faster.

In 2009 full-body suits made entirely of polyurethane were introduced. These compressing, seamless suits allowed swimmers to glide on the top of the water where there is less drag, thereby boosting speed significantly. Many swimmers wore them in the 2009 World Championships. Phelps did not.

Because these suits so enhanced a swimmer's performance, they caused a controversy. As of May 2010, these full- body suits were banned from swimming. Male swimmers can wear waist-to-knee suits. Females can wear shoulder-to-knee suits.

incredible strength to get through his schedule. Even if he did, many things could go wrong, most of which were out of his control.

For instance, he was scheduled to swim in three relay events. To win a gold medal in these events, every member of the team had to be at their best. Ill health, a false start, which occurs when a swimmer accidentally starts before the starting signal, or a faulty turn by just one swimmer could lose the race for the team. According to journalist Susan Casey, "There were many spots where Phelps—who described the competition's nine days as 'nothing but an upward roller coaster'—could've seen his ride derailed. Seventeen races in eight events, three of which were relays, meant 38 opportunities for false starts, countless chances for stroke or turn violations."[71]

Negative Remarks

With the odds stacked against him, it is not surprising that many people predicted Phelps would fail. Among the most vocal were the Australian press and Phelps's long time rival Ian Thorpe. "I don't think he can do it, but I'd love to see it," Thorpe said. "There's a thing called competition. There won't just be one athlete competing and in a lot of events, he has a lot of strong competition."[72]

Ian Thorpe, a former Australian swimming champion, watches at the 2008 Olympic Games in Beijing as Michael Phelps defies the odds and becomes the first ever eight-time gold medalist.

Knowing how Phelps reacted to a challenge, Bowman made sure Phelps saw every negative article. Phelps posted them in his locker. Seeing them fired him up. Indeed, the negative comments helped him to overcome the obstacles ahead of him.

Taking on Challenges

Just as the experts predicted, things did go wrong. Phelps's performance in the 200-meter butterfly is one of the most amazing in Olympic history. Early in the race, his goggles filled with water and he was swimming blind. He had to count his strokes to keep from smashing into the wall. He recalls, "They started filling up more and more. And about 75 meters left in the race, I could see nothing. I couldn't see the black line. I couldn't see the T [a large black "T" at the bottom of the pool that warns swimmers they are

approaching the wall]. I couldn't see anything. I was purely going by stroke count. And I couldn't take my goggles off because they were underneath two swim caps."[73] Phelps still won the race, but he was disappointed that he had not swum faster.

Phelps's performance in the 100-meter butterfly is another incredible story. Going into the finals, his chief competitor for a gold medal was Serbia's Milorad Cavic. In the semifinal race, Cavic made a motion toward Phelps daring the American to beat him. It was an act, which people who knew Phelps, likened to poking a tiger with a stick. Phelps did not respond verbally, nor did his

It is a photo finish for U.S. swimmer Michael Phelps (right) and Serbia's Milorad Cavic during the men's 100-meter butterfly final at the 2008 Olympics. Phelps won the gold in a record time of 50:58.

face show any emotion. But he was angry. No way would he lose this race. Phelps's Olympic teammate Eric Vendt explains: "When it gets to be game time, you can see it in his face: 'I'm Michael Phelps and I'm not going to lose.' When push comes to shove, he is going to be there. I have never seen him lose a close race."[74]

The race, which was held on the eighth day of the games, did not start out well for Phelps. He was exhausted going into the event. After 50 meters, he was in seventh place. It looked like Cavic was going to win easily.

Then, with only 35 meters left in the race, Phelps came speeding back. As the swimmers reached the wall, Phelps and Cavic were tied for the lead. Thinking he had the race won, Cavic lifted his head out of the water before touching the wall. This slowed him down. Phelps thought he had lost. He had misjudged the finish and took an extra stroke. He did not know it, but the momentum that stroke generated was just what he needed to win. In a stunning photo finish, Phelps touched the wall one one-hundredth of a second before Cavic.

When he found out that he had won, Phelps smashed the water with his hand and let out a triumphant roar. He recalls: "I was like, 'Please get your hand to the wall first. Please get your hand to the wall first.' I remember like the last two or three strokes that I had misjudged the finish. I thought that was the race. As soon as I hit the wall, I saw I had won. I looked up, and saw it was by one one-hundredth. And you know that's where the emotions came out. You know, that's where the big splash in the water, like the big roar. I mean you could tell that I was pretty intense after that race."[75]

Another verbal challenge, this time in the 4x100-meter freestyle relay, also got Phelps's competitive juices flowing. This time French swimmer, Alain Bernard, who was the world 100-meter-freestyle record holder, announced to the media that the French swimmers were going to smash the Americans

Phelps had never before competed internationally in a race where he swam the 100-meter freestyle. But Bernard's announcement got him motivated. Every member of the team, including Phelps, swam well. But so did the French. When Jason Lezak, the final American swimmer, jumped into the water, the Americans were behind. In a dramatic performance, Lezak managed to make up the distance, beating the French by .08 of a second. When Lezak touched the wall, Phelps let out a joyous scream.

Phelps managed to defy the odds. He won all of his final races, set seven world records, and hit his personal goal time in all but two events, the 100- and 200-meter butterfly.

Bringing Swimming into the Spotlight

Just as Phelps had hoped, the 2008 Olympics was the most watched televised event in American history. Approximately 250 million Americans tuned in to the games. Many watched just to see Phelps swim.

NBC.com counted 1.3 billion hits to their Olympics Web page and 75 million hits to their video clips. Phelps generated 20 percent of this Web traffic. Phelps's performance sparked so much interest that his final race was shown live on the Jumbo Tron at a Baltimore Ravens football game. Even basketball greats Kobe Bryant and LeBron James, who were in Beijing with the U.S. Olympic basketball team, couldn't resist watching Phelps swim. They attended two of his events and stayed to watch him receive his eighth gold medal. According to sportswriter Alan Shipnuck:

> Debbie Phelps's son turned the Beijing Olympics into a serialized thriller with nightly installments that played out in prime time. Eight gold medals and seven world records would have been more than enough to secure his stardom, but Phelps's performance was made all the more unforgettable by two images for the ages: his primal scream punctuating an improbable U.S. comeback in the 4x100-meter freestyle relay on the second night of coverage, and the heart-stopping, fingertip-bending photo finish in the 100 butterfly for his penultimate gold. In the midst of a contentious presidential election and the first signs of a faltering economy, Phelps brought Americans together by the tens of millions, the TV serving as a portal to a faraway land and the outer limit of athletic achievement. As a spectator sport swimming has always resided in the margins,

and even during the Olympics it is often overshadowed by gymnastics and track. But in China, Phelps turned his every race into can't miss television.[76]

"The Greatest Athlete in the World"

Phelps's spectacular achievement in the Olympics turned him into a superstar. People all over the world were awed by his perform-ance. Many agreed with Phelps's teammate Brennan Hansen when he told the press: "What he did . . . beats winning the Tour de France, beats making the last putt at the U.S. Open. This guy is the greatest athlete in the world and every athlete in the world needs to tip their hats to this guy."[77]

Phelps's life became a blur of nonstop touring. He was mobbed wherever he went. Young women screamed at the sight of him. He hosted *Saturday Night Live*, rang the opening bell at the New York Stock Exchange, was a presenter on the MTV Video Awards, received honors from the Maryland Senate, and was named *Sports Illustrated*'s 2008 Sportsman of the Year. He received so many

Olympic gold medalist Michael Phelps (left) poses with singer Kid Rock at the 2008 MTV Video Awards in Los Angeles, California, on September 7, 2008.

Michael Phelps's Diet

While he is training, Michael Phelps burns approximately 1000 calories per hour. In comparison, an average man exercising for an hour by walking briskly burns about 200 calories. To replenish the calories he burns; to maintain, recover, and repair his overworked muscles; and to have enough energy to keep training, Phelps eats 10,000 to 12,000 calories per day. An average man needs to eat about 2000 calories per day.

Phelps's diet has a high level of complex carbohydrates, which give the body energy. His typical breakfast consists of three fried egg sandwiches with cheese, tomatoes, lettuce, and fried onions, three chocolate chip pancakes, a five-egg omelet, a bowl of grits, three slices of French toast, and two cups of coffee. This meal alone contains about 3000 calories.

For lunch he eats 1 pound (0.5 kg) of pasta with tomato sauce and two ham and cheese sandwiches accompanied by 1000 calories of energy drinks. Dinner includes another pound of pasta with tomato sauce, a large pizza, and 1000 calories of energy drinks.

A similar diet would be unhealthy for most people, and really hard to consume.

sponsorship deals that his agent predicted his lifetime earnings would top $100 million. Through it all, he remained modest. "It makes me feel good," he says about being called the greatest athlete in the world. "[But] I don't think of myself as that. I just think of myself as, honestly, a normal person coming in here, swimming every day because I love it. I just have high goals for myself and I don't give up until I achieve those."[78]

Making Swimming More Popular

Besides making him a superstar, his performance at the Olympics helped him to achieve his long-term goal of raising the public's interest in swimming. Since the Olympics, more young people are taking up the sport. In 2008 USA Swimming recorded a 12.2 percent increase in membership, its largest increase in twenty-nine years, and an 11.2 percent increase in 2009. Not only that, professional swimmers are earning endorsement deals that are comparable to those of other elite athletes, which is unprecedented. And because so many viewers tuned in to see Phelps swim during the Olympics, for the first time ever NBC televised live coverage of the 2009 swimming World Championships in Rome and the 2009 U.S. Nationals. It will air the 2010, and 2011 U.S. Nationals. According to Mike McCarley, vice president for NBC Sports' Olympic division, " Michael has taken swimming to a new level."[79]

Going Home

The combination of the Olympics and the public appearances that followed exhausted Phelps, so he decided to take some time off from swimming. He and Bowman both returned to Baltimore. Phelps moved into a four-story condominium looking out on the city's harbor. And he and Bowman became partners in Aquatic Ventures, a company that owns controlling shares in the NBAC. The two plan to remodel the seventy-eight-year-old facility, which is small and run down. According to Phelps, "We want to turn it into one of the best places to train in the country. We want to attract the best swimmers, have the best facilities, the best environment."[80]

Phelps is not just interested in providing the best environment for elite swimmers. He is working to expand access to swimming pools and swimming lessons for everyone, which, he hopes, will reduce childhood deaths by drowning and increase participation in the sport. One way he is doing this is through the Michael Phelps Foundation. It gives money to programs that promote water safety and youth swimming. Phelps started the foundation with $1 million of his own money. He explains: "For me to be able to welcome other kids and share the experiences that I've had for the past 15 years of my life, it's something that I think is important and something that will be fun. . . . I hope [the foundation] will help me inspire others to achieve their dreams and [also help me] give back to the sport that has given me so much."[81]

Olympic gold medalist Michael Phelps talks to children at the Boys and Girls Club of Burbank on September 8, 2008. Phelps is talking with children to promote water safety and youth swimming.

Only Too Human

By 2008 Phelps appeared to be achieving all his goals. Then, he made a terrible mistake. Early in 2009 he attended a party where he was photographed holding a marijuana pipe. On February 1, 2009, the picture was released to the media. It was plastered all over the Internet, newspapers, and television, creating quite a scandal. The local sheriff started an investigation, but there was not enough evidence for any legal actions. This was not the kind of publicity Phelps wanted to bring to swimming.

Although Phelps had always tested drug free for swimming events and had broken no USA Swimming rule, because of the poor example he had set for the many young people who looked up to him, the organization suspended him from all competitions for three months. Phelps accepted the punishment without complaint. He believed he deserved it.

This was the lowest point in Phelps's life. He felt as if he had let down his family, his coach, his friends, his fans, and the sport he loved. Phelps anguished over whether he should keep swimming at all. He worried that his presence would hurt the sport. "I had no idea really what to do," he explains. "I knew that I'd made a mistake. And I know that when you do make a mistake you're responsible for all of the consequences."[82]

Phelps was too confused and depressed to train regularly. When he did, he swam for only a few minutes before returning home. Bowman did not think Phelps should retire from swimming until he was tired of competing. "I was not really concerned whether he would quit or not," Bowman explains. "But I did think it would be bad if he walked away because of this thing. He should go on his own terms."[83]

To motivate Phelps, Bowman sent him text messages consisting only of goal times. This went on for a few months. Finally, Phelps texted back that no one could go that fast. This was when Bowman knew Phelps had taken the bait and would keep swimming.

For his part, Phelps made a list of the pros and cons of swimming and quitting. Swimming won out. Michael was back.

Back in the Pool

Phelps began training with a vengeance. But he had missed six months of intensive training. Considering that it takes about two days in the pool for an elite swimmer to make up for every missed day, he had a lot of catching up to do. When his suspension ended in May 2009, he was 20 pounds (9.09kg) thinner than he had been in Beijing and was still getting back into racing shape. Yet, he managed to set two individual world records and win five gold medals and one silver medal in the 2009 World Championships in Rome.

In the 100-meter butterfly, Phelps became the first man ever to swim the event in under 50 seconds, coming in at 49.82 seconds. This victory was particularly sweet because Phelps once again beat Milorad Cavic. Despite electronic and photographic evidence to the contrary, Cavic loudly insisted that he had beat Phelps in the event in Beijing. He went on to talk trash, daring Phelps to beat him in Rome. That, of course, was all the motivation Phelps needed.

Michael Phelps holds up his fist in celebration after winning the gold medal for the men's 100-meter butterfly at the 2009 World Championships in Rome on August 1, 2009.

Into the Future

With the World Championships behind him, Phelps is focused on the 2012 Olympics. His goal sheet is secret. It is likely he will drop some events and add others. He is showing an interest in swimming short sprint events, which presents him with a new challenge.

Beyond the 2012 Olympics, the future is wide open for Phelps. Currently, he says he will retire after the games, but that could change. Because he loves working with children, it is possible he will become a swimming coach. In 2009 he wrote a children's book, *How to Train with a T. Rex and Win 8 Gold Medals*. He may write others in the future. Or he may become a full-time businessman. He and Bowman are considering expanding Aquatic Ventures to other cities. Of course, Phelps plans to continue raising water safety awareness and working with his foundation.

"There are still things that I want to achieve and that I want to accomplish,"[84] he says. Although those things might be secret, it is likely that by setting goals and working hard, Phelps will achieve them.

Introduction: "Dream It, Believe It, Work at It, Go for It"

1. Michael Phelps with Alan Abrahamson, *No Limits*. New York: Free Press, 2008, p. 14.
2. Vicki Michaelis, "Built to Swim, Phelps Found a Refuge in the Water," *USA Today*, July 31, 2008. www.usatoday.com/sports/olympics/beijing/swimming/2008-07-31-phelps_N.htm.
3. Michael Phelps with Alan Abrahamson, *No Limits*, p. 38.
4. Debbie Phelps with Mim Eichler Rivas, *A Mother for All Seasons*. New York: HarperCollins, 2009, p. 261.
5. Michael Phelps with Alan Abrahamson, *No Limits*, p. 132.
6. Michael Phelps with Brian Cazeneuve, *Beneath the Surface*. Champaign, IL: Sports Publishing, 2008, p. 158.
7. Mike Celizic, "Phelps Did Something Common, Not Evil," *NBC Sports*, February 4, 2009. http://openmike.msnbc.msn.com/archive/2009/02/04/1781379.aspx.
8. Quoted in "Michael Phelps on Making Olympic History," *60 Minutes* interview with Anderson Cooper, *CBS News*, November 25, 2008. http://www.cbsnews.com/stories/2008/11/25/60minutes/main4633123.shtml.
9. Michael Phelps with Alan Abrahamson, *No Limits*, p. 18.

Chapter 1: A Safe Haven

10. Debbie Phelps with Mim Eichler Rivas, *A Mother for All Seasons*, p. 92.
11. Michael Phelps with Brian Cazeneuve, *Beneath the Surface*, p. 13.
12. Michael Phelps with Brian Cazeneuve, *Beneath the Surface*, p. 12.
13. Debbie Phelps with Mim Eichler Rivas, *A Mother for All Seasons*, p. 126.
14. "Michael Phelps," Tavis Smiley Interview, *PBS.org*, December 11, 2008. www.pbs.org/kcet/tavissmiley/archive/200812/20081211_phelps.html.

15. Michael Phelps with Brian Cazeneuve, *Beneath the Surface*, p. 14.

16. "Twenty Questions for Whitney (Phelps) Flickinger," *USA Swimming*, 2004. http://www.usaswimming.org/USASWeb/ViewMiscArticle.aspx?TabId=280&Alias=rainbow&Lang=en&mid=408&ItemId=2925.

17. Quoted in Bob Schaller, *Michael Phelps: The Untold Story of a Champion*. New York: St. Martin's Press, 2008, p. 6.

18. Quoted in Schaller, *Michael Phelps: The Untold Story of a Champion*, p. 5.

19. Michael Phelps with Brian Cazeneuve, *Beneath the Surface*, p. 16.

20. Quoted in Lauren Passell, "Mom to Live By: Debbie Phelps," *Parenting*. http://www.parenting.com/article/Mom/Work--Family/Mom-to-Live-By-Debbie-Phelps.

21. Michael Phelps with Alan Abrahamson, *No Limits*, p. 20.

22. Quoted in Rick Reilly, "Water Boy," *Sports Illustrated* Vault, August 30, 2004. http://sportsillustrated.cnn.com/vault/article/magazine/MAG1106346/index.htm.

Chapter 2: "When the Student Is Ready, the Teacher Appears"

23. Quoted in Passell, "Mom to Live By: Debbie Phelps."

24. Michael Phelps with Brian Cazeneuve, *Beneath the Surface*, p. 23.

25. Debbie Phelps with Mim Eichler Rivas, *A Mother for All Seasons*, p. 168.

26. Quoted in Amy Shipley, "Bowman, Phelps Have Golden Partnership," *Washington Post*, January 23, 2009. www.washingtonpost.com/wp-dyn/content/article/2009/01/22/AR2009012204122.html.

27. Michael Phelps with Brian Cazeneuve, *Beneath the Surface*, p. 27.

28. Michael Phelps with Alan Abrahamson, *No Limits*, p. 62.

29. Michael Phelps with Alan Abrahamson, *No Limits*, p. 70.

30. Michael Phelps with Alan Abrahamson, *No Limits*, p. 69.

31. Quoted in Ian Stafford, "I Used to Hate Getting My Face Wet," *Daily Mail* (London), May 31, 2008. http://www.dailymail.co.uk/sport/othersports/article-1023288/I-used-hate-getting-face-wet-says-swimmer-chasing-Olympic-golds.html.

32. Michael Phelps with Alan Abrahamson, *No Limits*, p. 18.

33. Debbie Phelps with Mim Eichler Rivas, *A Mother for All Seasons*, p. 170.
34. Debbie Phelps with Mim Eichler Rivas, *A Mother for All Seasons*, p. 172.
35. "Michael Phelps," Tavis Smiley Interview.
36. Quoted in Kevin Van Valkenburg, "Opposites Attract," *WQAD*, August 16, 2008. www.wqad.com/bal-te.sp.bowman16aug 16,0,215788.story.
37. Quoted in Schaller, *Michael Phelps: The Untold Story of a Champion*, p. 25.
38. Quoted in "Bob Bowman: Man of Many Talents," *NBC Olympics.com*, August 5, 2008. http://www.2008.nbcolympics .com/swimming/news/newsid=167130.html#bob+bowman+ man+many+talents.
39. Quoted in "Bob Bowman: Man of Many Talents."
40. Quoted in "Bob Bowman: Man of Many Talents."
41. Quoted in Michaelis, "Built to Swim, Phelps Found a Refuge in the Water."

Chapter 3: "The Motivation Machine"

42. "Michael Phelps," Tavis Smiley Interview.
43. Michael Phelps with Alan Abrahamson, *No Limits*, p. 22.
44. "Michael Phelps," Tavis Smiley Interview.
45. Michael Phelps with Brian Cazeneuve, *Beneath the Surface*, p. 4.
46. Quoted in Superstar Interview: Michael Phelps," *Parenting*. www.parenting.com/article/Mom/Work--Family/Superstar-Interview-Michael-Phelps/2.
47. Quoted in Alan Abrahamson, "Built to Succeed and Assume His Place in History," *NBC Sports*, August 17, 2008. www.2008 .nbcolympics.com/swimming/news/newsid=206302.html.
48. Quoted in "Michael Phelps' ADHD Has Not Stopped Him from Success," *Edge Foundation*. http://www.edgefoundation .org/blog/2008/08/15/michael-phelpss-adhd-is-not-an-attention-deficit/.
49. Quoted in Scott Gummer, "The Swiminator," *USA Weekend*, August 8, 2004. http://159.54.226.237/04_issues/04080 8/040808olympics.html.

50. Quoted in Michaelis, "Built to Swim, Phelps Found a Refuge in the Water."
51. Michael Phelps with Alan Abrahamson, *No Limits*, p. 80.
52. Michael Phelps with Brian Cazeneuve, *Beneath the Surface*, p. 203.
53. Quoted in Debbie Phelps with Mim Eichler Rivas, *A Mother for All Seasons*, p. 218.
54. Schaller, *Michael Phelps: The Untold Story of a Champion*, p. 41.

Chapter 4: Ups and Downs

55. Michael Phelps with Alan Abrahamson, *No Limits*, p. 121.
56. Michael Phelps with Brian Cazeneuve, *Beneath the Surface*, p. 231.
57. Quoted in Vicki Michaelis, "Olympic Star Michael Phelps Charged with Drunken Driving," *USA Today*, November 8, 2005. www.usatoday.com/sports/olympics/summer/2004-11-08-phelps-arrest_x.htm.
58. Michael Phelps with Brian Cazeneuve, *Beneath the Surface*, p. 235.
59. Quoted in Associated Press, "Olympic Standout Phelps Arrested for DUI," *NBC Sports*, November 10, 2004. http://nbcsports.msnbc.com/id/6437288/.
60. Quoted in David Hancock, "Olympic Champ Sentenced for DUI," *CBS News*, December 29, 2004. www.cbsnews.com/stories/2004/11/08/national/main654380.shtml.
61. Michael Phelps with Brian Cazeneuve, *Beneath the Surface*, p. 165.
62. Quoted in Schaller, *Michael Phelps: The Untold Story of a Champion*, p. 46.
63. Michael Phelps with Brian Cazeneuve, *Beneath the Surface*, p. 251.
64. Quoted in "Superstar Interview: Michael Phelps."
65. Quoted in Abrahamson, "Built to Succeed and Assume His Place in History."
66. Quoted in Abrahamson, "Built to Succeed and Assume His Place in History."
67. Quoted in Brian Cazeneuve, "Mind Boggling," *Sports Illustrated*

Vault, August 9, 2007. http://sportsillustrated.cnn.com/vault/
article/magazine/MAG1108536/index.htm.

68. Debbie Phelps with Mim Eichler Rivas, *A Mother for All Seasons*, p. 244.

69. Quoted in "Superstar Interview: Michael Phelps."

Chapter 5: Changing Swimming Forever

70. Quoted in Karen Crouse, "Phelps Wants to Help Swimming Grow," *New York Times*, August 18, 2008. http://swimming.about.com/b/2008/09/20/michael-phelps-wants-to-help-swimming-grow.htm.

71. Susan Casey, "We Are All Witnesses," *Sports Illustrated* Vault, August 25, 2008. http://sportsillustrated.cnn.com/vault/article/mag azine/MAG1144316/index.htm.

72. Quoted in Michael Phelps with Brian Cazeneuve, *Beneath the Surface*, p. 281.

73. Quoted in "Michael Phelps on Making Olympic History."

74. Quoted in Abrahamson, "Built to Succeed and Assume His Place in History."

75. Quoted in "Michael Phelps on Making Olympic History."

76. Alan Shipnuck, "Sportsman of the Year," *Sports Illustrated*, December 8, 2008, p. 42.

77. Quoted in Pat Forde, "An Embodiment of the Olympic Idea, Michael Phelps Saved the Games," *ESPN*, August 17, 2008. http://espn.go.com/oly/summer08/story?columnist=forde_pat&id=359324.

78. Quoted in Mike Celizic, "Michael Phelps: Greatest Olympian Ever?" *MSNBC*, June 27, 2008. www.msnbc.msn.com/id/25396030/.

79. Quoted in Brain Cazeneuve, "Water Under the Bridge," *SI* Vault, May 25, 2009. http://vault.sportsillustrated.cnn.com/vault/article/magazine/MAG1155653/index.htm.

80. Quoted in Shipnuck, "Sportsman of the Year," p. 42.

81. Quoted in Bob Considine, "Phelps to Use $1 Million Bonus to Start Charity," *MSNBC*, September 2, 2008. www.msnbc.msn.com/id/26506320.

82. Quoted in Mike Celizic, "Phelps: It Was a Bad Mistake," *MSNBC*, March 13, 2009. www.msnbc.msn.com/id/29683665/.

83. Quoted in Associated Press, "Phelps Returns, Ready to Race Again," *Las Cruces (NM) Sun News*, May 6, 2009, p. 4B.
84. Quoted in Celizic, "Phelps: It Was a Bad Mistake."

Important Dates

1985
Michael Phelps is born on June 30.

1992
Phelps's parents separate. He learns to swim.

1997
Bob Bowman becomes Phelps's coach.

2000
Phelps competes in the Olympics.

2001
Phelps breaks two world records. He receives the American Swimmer of the Year award and becomes a professional swimmer.

2002
For the second year in a row, Phelps breaks two world records and receives the American Swimmer of the Year award.

2003
Phelps breaks eight world records. He wins four gold and two silver medals at the World Championships. He receives the USAA Athlete of the Year, World Championship Swimmer of the Meet, American and World Swimmer of the Year awards.

2004
Phelps is arrested for driving under the influence. He breaks two world records. He wins six gold and two bronze medals in the Olympics. He receives the Golden Goggles Male Performance and Male Athlete, the American and World Swimmer of the Year, and USOC Sportsman of the Year awards. His autobiography *Beneath the Surface* is published.

2005
Phelps earns five gold and one silver medal at the World Cham-

pionships. He receives ESPY's Best Olympic Performance and the Teen Choice Athlete of the Year awards.

2006

Phelps breaks three world records. He receives the Golden Goggle Male Performance and Relay Performance, and World and American Swimmer of the Year awards.

2007

Phelps breaks six world records. He earns seven gold medals at the World Championships. He receives the Golden Goggle Male Performance, Relay Performance, and Male Athlete of the Year, World and American Swimmer of the Year, and World Championships Swimmer of the Meet Awards.

2008

Phelps breaks nine world records. He becomes the first person to earn eight gold medals in one Olympics. He receives the Golden Goggle Male Performance, Relay Performance, and Male Athlete of the Year; World and American Swimmer of the Year; and USOC Sportsman of the Year awards. He is named *Sports Illustrated*'s Sportsman of the Year. He starts the Michael Phelps Foundation. His second autobiography, *No Limits*, is published.

2009

Phelps is photographed holding a marijuana pipe. He is suspended from competition for three months. He starts Aqua Ventures with Bowman. He breaks five world records. He wins five gold and one silver medal at the World Championships. He receives the World Championships Swimmer of the Meet and the ESPY Male Athlete, Championship Performance, Record Breaking Performance, and U.S. Male Olympian awards. His children's book *How to Train with a T. Rex and Win 8 Gold Medals* is published.

For More Information

Books

Virginia Fox, *History of Swimming*. Farmington Hills, MI: Lucent Books, 2003. This book covers the history of competitive swimming.

Meish Goldish, *Michael Phelps: Anything Is Possible*. New York: Bearport, 2009. This is a simple book about Phelps's life.

Sue Macy, *Swifter, Higher, Stronger: A Photographic History of the Summer Olympics*. Washington, DC: National Geographic Children's Books, 2008. This book gives a broad history of the Summer Olympics with a look at memorable athletes such as Michael Phelps and Mark Spitz. It has great photos.

David Torsiello, *Michael Phelps: Swimming for Olympic Gold*. Berkeley Heights, NJ: Enslow, 2009. A brief biography of Phelps.

Periodicals

Brian Cazeneuve, "End of an Era," *Sports Illustrated*, August 10, 2009, p. 31.

Paul Newberry, "Phelps' Suspension Ends; He's Ready to Race" *Albuquerque (NM) Journal*, May 6, 2009, p. B5.

Alan Shipnuck, "Sportsman of the Year," *Sports Illustrated*, December 8, 2008, p. 40–48.

Web Sites

Michael Phelps (www.michaelphelps.com/2004/english.html) This is Michael Phelps's official Facebook page.

Michael Phelps.info (www.michaelphelps.info/). This fan site has lots of news, photos, and videos.

MSNBC, "Michael Phelps" (www.msnbc.msn.com/?id=11881 780 &q=michael%20phelps&p=1&st=1&sm=user). Links to articles and videos about Phelps.

NBC Sports, "NBC Beijing 2008" (www.2008.nbcolympics .com/index.html). Videos and information about the 2008 Olympics with lots on Phelps.

Swim Room.com, "Michael Phelps" (www.swimroom.com/phelps). This is Phelps's page on the Swim Room Web site. It contains news, photos, his blog, and videos.

Twitter, "The Swim Channel" (http://twitter.com/TheSwim Channel). Tweets from many professional swimmers, including Phelps, are posted here.

USA Swimming (www.usaswimming.org/usasweb/Desktop Default.aspx). The official Web site of USA Swimming offers information about swim clubs, meets, swimmers (including Phelps), and swimming news.

Picture Credits

Barbara Sheen is the author of more than fifty books for young people. She lives in New Mexico with her family. She has been a swimmer all her life. She even swims in her dreams!!